PUSHING
BACK THE
DARKNESS

D1565671

PUSHING BACK THE DARKNESS

MELISSA R. RICH, LMFT, Ph.D.

METROPOLITAN LIBRARY SYSTEM
"SERVING OKLAHOMA COUNTY"

TATE PUBLISHING
AND ENTERPRISES, LLC

Pushing Back the Darkness
Copyright © 2014 by Melissa R. Rich, LMFT, Ph.D. All rights reserved.

No part of this publication may be reproduced, stored in a retrieval system or transmitted in any way by any means, electronic, mechanical, photocopy, recording or otherwise without the prior permission of the author except as provided by USA copyright law.

The opinions expressed by the author are not necessarily those of Tate Publishing, LLC.

Published by Tate Publishing & Enterprises, LLC
127 E. Trade Center Terrace | Mustang, Oklahoma 73064 USA
1.888.361.9473 | www.tatepublishing.com

Tate Publishing is committed to excellence in the publishing industry. The company reflects the philosophy established by the founders, based on Psalm 68:11,
"The Lord gave the word and great was the company of those who published it."

Book design copyright © 2014 by Tate Publishing, LLC. All rights reserved.
Cover design by Rtor Maghuyop
Interior design by Mary Jean Archival

Published in the United States of America

ISBN: 978-1-63185-316-6
1. Self-Help / Mood Disorders/ Depression
2. Self-Help / Personal Growth / Happiness
14.06.11

This book is lovingly dedicated to the memory of my late husband, Ed Rich, who struggled with the octopus most of his life but is now, joyously and fully, living in the light.

Contents

Section 8—Things that Can Help – Spiritual

Section 9—All the Rest

How It Began

In some ways becoming a Christian therapist was inevitable for me. I am the oldest of five siblings, so I grew up taking care of others. My parents pastored churches and served as missionaries in Latin America, sometimes both at the same time. So I grew up in spiritual settings where it was very common to see my father and/ or mother encouraging, advising, and comforting others on a regular basis.

I also learned about confidentiality at a very early age. I would hear my parents discussing a family in the church and would be told, "What you hear stays in our home, it's not to be discussed elsewhere." We all grew up understanding and respecting that. I knew that what my parents did helped other people, and I believed it had great value.

My temperament was also a factor—I am very stable emotionally (to the point where sometimes I think I'm boring!), and I tend to look at things objectively. I have always believed that God blessed me with a great deal of common sense as well as a certain amount of intelligence. I like working with people and enjoy helping them.

Interestingly enough, however, mercy is *not* one of my spiritual gifts. I have some, just not a lot. Mom used to ask me, "How did you get to be a therapist without any mercy?" I prefer to think of myself as a practical, hands-on counselor. I usually try to figure out what the problem is, what has worked and what has not, and how to make the situation better. That can be done without a lot of mercy—common sense works just fine!

One of the things I began to see very early on, however, is that people suffering from depression didn't respond well to helpful counsel. In fact, they often didn't respond to *any* type of treatment. This was puzzling, especially early in my career. With the naïveté of youth and inexperience I couldn't figure why these people didn't follow my excellent suggestions and just get better!

It took years of working as a therapist for me to realize that depression is a complicated, multilayered issue that, as my sons would say, *is a tricky beast.* Over the twenty-five-plus years that I have been counseling, I would estimate that depression has been a factor in 60–70 percent of the cases I have seen. It wasn't always the main issue (thankfully!), but it was often present in some form. When depression was the main complaint, the clients typically only came in a few times, and I was forced to admit that my best efforts had not been very helpful.

There were exceptions—clients who did make significant improvements—and I began to observe the factors they had in common. I'll talk about what helped them recover later in this book. But over time, it became clear to me that depressed clients were in a different category and needed something extra to help them get better. I was beginning to amass some helpful tools and techniques, but frustratingly, clients still weren't getting much better. Either they wouldn't follow my suggestions, or they dropped out of therapy after a few sessions, and I never learned how they turned out.

At the age of twenty-six, I did something that would give me a much closer, in-depth understanding of depression than I had ever wanted. I married Ed.

Life with Ed

Ed was a good, funny, smart, kind Christian man—but not a happy one. I didn't realize it at the time we met, but he had battled depression off and on for most of his life. When we met, in the singles group of our church, he was doing pretty well emotionally. I know now that many people with depression are able to hide it from others. (I had one downcast client tell me that nobody really knew her because she wore a mask all the time.) During our courtship and the early years of our marriage, Ed was probably functioning at his best—it was only later that things deteriorated badly.

I look back now and see patterns and red flags that weren't apparent at the time. After a couple of years of marriage, I realized that he was a very negative, pessimistic person. However, partly because this was so foreign to me, I kept telling myself that when (fill in the blank) occurred, he'd be happier. Somewhere around the fifteenth year of our twenty-nine-year marriage, it dawned on me that this wasn't accurate, and I realized a sobering truth—Ed would never be happy.

This was a very hard pill for me to swallow. By temperament, I am an optimistic, positive person who has been blessed with a loving, stable upbringing. My family and I had our disagreements, but I never once doubted that they loved me or would help if I needed them. I couldn't understand Ed's negativity. He was blessed with a good education, a great career (a dentist), good friends, a solid church with sound biblical teaching, terrific family—what more did he need? It made no sense to me.

I am forever grateful that he was at his best during our sons David and Josh's early lives. During their formative years (till they were about eleven and nine), he was at his best—coaching their various sports teams, serving as chairman of the deacons, active in choir and drama, going on mission trips, and generally functioning very well. Because they were so young, they don't remember a lot of that, but the steady foundation we were able to lay helped them become the stable, well-rounded young men they are today.

Ed's real deterioration began in May 2000. I remember it very well because the precipitating factor was that he built a new dental office. Prior to that time, he rented a small building where he could oversee everything—and as I'll get to later, control was a huge issue for him. The new building was beautiful and bigger, and he could no longer micromanage everything—although not for lack of trying! That was when he felt things begin to slip out of control, and his depression came roaring back.

Ed's depression took a heavy toll on our marriage. As he began to withdraw physically from people and events in our lives, I began to pull away from him emotionally. In the beginning, I didn't have a clear picture of what was happening, but I knew we had two young sons and a household to run. Someone had to be functioning, and since Ed was barely managing to keep his head above water, that left me.

I'd known for some time that Ed's thinking and perspective were skewed, but until he built his new building and things spiraled out of control for him, I had no idea how much. For years, he would make odd remarks that had me shaking my head in puzzlement. His dental office took a small hit in income, and he told me in all seriousness that he was afraid we would lose our house. We had money in savings and investments, but he was afraid we wouldn't be able to pay our taxes. I really didn't attach much importance to his remarks because they seemed like random comments here and there. After a while, things would improve, and he would get back to "normal." Now I know that his thinking was never normal. He was just able to pretend that it was for a long time.

As I said before, I made excuses for him for years. I truly did not understand the depths of his insecurity and how his years of depression had slanted his reasoning. Ed was the oldest of three children, and his parents went through a bitter divorce when he was about eight. As the firstborn, he was the most aware of what was going on and appeared to be the most affected by their fighting and anger. I believe this contributed to his emotional issues later in life. As with many children of divorce, this event had a profound impact on Ed, and I'm not sure he was ever fully able to work through it. However, I have always been deeply grateful that he made a huge effort to *not* pass any of his dysfunction on to our sons. He spent an enormous amount of emotional energy giving them a stable, loving, and secure foundation, and I deeply appreciate his efforts.

I'm sad to say that the last ten years of Ed's life were pretty miserable for him, and I couldn't do anything about it. It was the supreme irony; he was married to a family therapist, and I couldn't make him any happier. I realized, however, as much as I wanted to help him, Ed's unhappiness was his own responsibility. Ed puzzled those who knew him by his behavior. He would do something that made him feel a little better (exercise, journal, interact with people) and would comment on the fact that he felt healthier—and would never do the activity again! Over and over again, he would fall into this pattern. Finally the boys and I stopped believing him when he told us he was going to start an exercise program or join a particular group. We would offer verbal support and encouragement, but privately we knew that it wouldn't last—we had seen it too many times before.

I watched Ed sabotage himself for years—he would continue doing things that made him unhappy and would stop doing things that made him happy. It was exactly what Paul described: "I do not understand what I do. For what I want to do I do not do, but what I hate I do" (Rom. 7:15, niv).

What really puzzled me was that he was a very smart man—he was a doctor who often prescribed the very things for his patients that he was attempting to do. He knew these activities had value, so why didn't he do them?

Putting the Pieces Together

About a year after he died, I finally began to see all the pieces of the puzzle. I realized that Ed had obsessive compulsive personality disorder (OCPD). This is different from obsessive compulsive disorder (OCD). OCD is an anxiety disorder in which people have unwanted and repeated thoughts, feelings, ideas, sensations (obsessions), or behaviors that make them feel driven to do something (compulsions).

Often the person carries out the behaviors to get rid of the obsessive thoughts, but this only provides temporary relief. Not performing the obsessive rituals can cause great anxiety. OCD sufferers do things like washing their hands thirty times a day, checking the front door lock twenty times before leaving the house, being careful not to step on cracks, etc.

The *DSM-V* gives the following criteria for OCPD:

A pervasive pattern of preoccupation with orderliness, perfectionism, and mental and interpersonal control, at the expense of flexibility, openness, and efficiency, beginning by early adulthood and present in a variety of contexts, as indicated by four (or more) of the following:

- is preoccupied with details, rules, lists, order, organization, or schedules to the extent that the major point of the activity is lost
- shows perfectionism that interferes with task completion (e.g., is unable to complete a project because his or her own overly strict standards are not met)
- is excessively devoted to work and productivity to the exclusion of leisure activities and friendships (not accounted for by obvious economic necessity)
- is over-conscientious, scrupulous, and inflexible about matters of morality, ethics, or values (not accounted for by cultural or religious identification)
- is unable to discard worn-out or worthless objects even when they have no sentimental value
- is reluctant to delegate tasks or to work with others unless they submit to exactly his or her way of doing things
- adopts a miserly spending style toward both self and others; money is viewed as something to be hoarded for future catastrophes
- shows rigidity and stubbornness

(*Diagnostic and Statistical Manual of Mental Disorders*, Fifth Edition)

Ed had seven of the eight criteria. I realized that he had a huge preoccupation with control. He tried (unsuccessfully) to control everything! When he was unable to do this, he became hugely depressed and anxious—eventually to the point where he was unable to function. I mean that literally. The last few years of his life he was unable to run his dental office and eventually had to sell his practice.

Endings and Beginnings

I was hopeful again. Maybe getting rid of his practice would solve the problem. I knew, from being married to a dentist for twenty-eight years, that dentistry is an extremely stressful occupation. It doesn't appear that way at first but consider the following:

- The average American dentist's overhead is 73 percent.
- Many people dread going to see their dentist— and let them know it!
- The average dentist requires a large staff to run their office. This staff is typically composed of young women who move, return to school, get sick, have babies, etc., so there is usually a large turnover.

- The average dentist works in a very small, dark, wet area—any mistake (the filling has a rough edge) can be felt and can be painful!
- Many dentists develop back problems from constantly leaning over.

You get the picture. Looking back, I can see that dentistry was probably the worst possible occupational choice for someone with Ed's temperament, but of course, we didn't know that at the time. I was greatly relieved when the practice sold because I was sure that this would seriously reduce Ed's stress and he would be happier. Wrong again.

What I failed to understand was that removing one source of stress relieved that particular issue but didn't address the root problem. When the practice was gone and Ed didn't have that to worry about, he simply found *other things* to obsess over.

Ed had been in and out of therapy for years, but it never helped much. I was always baffled by this because Ed really did want to get better and was a fairly acquiescent client. Once I figured out his diagnosis, I realized that the depression he had been treated for was a *symptom*, not the core issue. He never received treatment for his main concern, which was control.

Ed truly tried to control everything and everyone around him. When his efforts were not successful, he became extremely negative, depressed, and withdrawn. I also realized that his thinking was almost completely black and white. In his mind, things were either perfect or horrible—there was no in-between. Since things were seldom perfect, they were usually horrible.

I think if Ed had received counseling for his desire to control people and events and had been able to change that desire, his depression would have significantly lessened. Conversely, if he had been able to actively do things (or stop doing things) that impacted his depression, he would have seen how illogical his thinking was and been able to change that. In Ed, as in many people, thinking/feeling/doing were extremely intertwined and were all involved in the depression that controlled his life. A positive change in any area would have affected the other areas as well.

Ed also regularly set himself up for disappointment and hurt by having extremely unrealistic expectations— and feeling angry and misused when they weren't met. He expected perfection in everything and everyone around him and couldn't seem to realize that we live in an imperfect world. I told him numerous times, "It doesn't work that way," in attempts to pacify and explain situations. His response was always, "But it should!" It would have been funny if it weren't so sad.

By the time he died, Ed had become an angry, frustrated, solitary, defeated, and hopeless individual. He was convinced he would never get better and nothing he could do would ever change that. Needless to say, his enjoyment of life was almost nonexistent. I felt horribly sorry for him but had no idea how to help him, especially because he *knew* what to do and consistently choose *not* to do it.

People have asked David, Josh, and me if we were sad when Ed died. Truthfully, none of us grieved for him very much. We miss him, but we all know that he is in heaven and is finally happy. It's sort of like watching someone you love take a long time to die of a particularly painful disease. Once they're gone, you're relieved—they're not suffering anymore. That's how we all felt.

To be honest, we were all relieved for ourselves as well. Once Ed was gone, it felt like a big, black cloud was lifted from our house. Since Ed became so reclusive toward the end and rarely (if ever) left the house, home was not a happy place for any of us. Let's face it, it's hard to watch someone you care about suffer, especially if you believe they're choosing to suffer needlessly. We all felt sorry for him but were also frustrated and confused.

Life without Ed has been much happier and simpler. Ed had a gift for complicating the simplest issue and overthinking everything (trying to control things again). He was aware of this and, at times, could even laugh about it. But he never seemed able to change it.

The best part of Ed being gone is that we all know we'll see him again one day. And when we do, he'll be the Ed he was always meant to be (and we'll be who we were meant to be as well). Our relationships with him will be healthy and well functioning. We'll all have been completed and made whole. I can't tell you how much I look forward to that!

Until then I'd like to do what I can to help other families deal with "the dark octopus." I visualize depression this way because it has so many tentacles, and they get into every aspect of an individual's life. I don't want Ed's experience to have been for nothing. I believe the worst thing we can do with mistakes is to waste them. We should look at them honestly, learn what we can, make amends if necessary and possible, let them go, and move on.

My approach to counseling is biblical based. That doesn't mean, however, that I have all the answers (I wish!). I don't understand why some people suffer from depression and others don't—it doesn't seem fair. Many people think that true Christians don't suffer from depression (or other emotional problems). I would love to believe this, but the evidence simply doesn't support it. And if it were true, the conversion rate to Christianity from depressed individuals would be overwhelming!

I don't believe everyone will be able to recover *fully* from depression, but I do believe everyone can get *significantly better*—if they are willing to work at it on a consistent basis. I know with certainty there is hope for recovery, but you have to be willing to dig in and do most of the work yourself. Just like losing weight, others can encourage and advise you, but they can't eat or exercise for you.

This book is my attempt to honor Ed's memory and have something good come out of his life. I think he would approve. My hope is that you can use what is in these pages to move toward recovery and push back the darkness that has been overtaking your life.

What Depression Is

Depression is one of those things that seems obvious but can be difficult to really understand. The *DSM-V* gives the following criteria for the two main types of depression.

Major Depressive Disorder

Five (or more) of the following symptoms have been present during the same two-week period and represent a change from previous functioning; at least one of the symptoms is either (1)) depressed mood, or (2) loss of interest or pleasure.

1. Depressed mood most of the day, nearly every day.
2. Markedly diminished interest or pleasure in all, or almost all, activities most of the day, nearly every day.

3. Significant weight loss when not dieting or weight gain, or decrease or increase in appetite nearly every day.
4. Insomnia or hypersomnia nearly every day.
5. Psychomotor agitation or retardation nearly every day.
6. Fatigue or loss of energy nearly every day.
7. Feelings of worthlessness or excessive or inappropriate guilt nearly every day.
8. Diminished ability to think or concentrate, or indecisiveness, nearly every day.
9. Recurrent thoughts of death (not just fear of dying), recurrent suicidal ideation without a specific plan, or a suicide attempt or a specific plan for committing suicide.

Persistent Depressive Disorder (Dysthymia)

1. Depressed mood for most of the day, for more days than not, for at least two years.
2. Presence, while depressed, of two (or more) of the following:
   a. Poor appetite or overeating
   b. Insomnia or hypersomnia
   c. Low energy or fatigue
   d. Low self-esteem
   e. Poor concentration or difficulty making decisions
   f. Feelings of hopelessness

Please note that I summarized the symptoms for both disorders. For an unabridged list of symptoms, please consult a *DSM*-V (*Diagnostic and Statistical Manual*-5).

The main distinctions between major depressive disorder (MDD) and persistent depressive disorder (PDD) are *severity and duration*. A major depressive disorder tends to have much more severe symptoms but typically doesn't last as long. As noted above, dysthymia can last for years, but the symptoms are more moderate. To make things even more confusing, an individual with PDD can periodically experience a major depressive episode. (I believe this is what happened to Ed on a regular basis.)

Depression is so prevalent that it's now referred to as "the common cold of mental illness." However, depression is not contagious, and sadly, you don't recover from it by resting a while or eating chicken soup. Here are some additional facts on depression that show why it is such a debilitating disorder:

- An estimated 350 million people worldwide suffer from depression.
- Depression is the leading cause of disability worldwide and is a major contributor to the global burden of disease.
- At its worst, depression can lead to suicide.
- Major depression is the leading cause of disability in the United States.
- Depression affects almost 10 percent of the population, or 19 million Americans, in a given year (this is one in ten adults).

- Women are affected by depression almost twice as often as men.
- The economic cost of depression is estimated to be over $30 billion each year.
- Two-thirds of those who are depressed never seek treatment and suffer needlessly.
- Research on twins suggests that there is a genetic component to the risk of developing depression.
- Research has also shown that the stress of a loss, especially the death of a loved one, may lead to depression in some people.

Depression is much more common in industrialized societies than in primitive ones. The blues were not nearly as prevalent in our grandparent's generations as they are in ours. My personal hypothesis on this is that getting more activity, sleep, sunlight, a better diet, and social connections helps inoculate against depression.

Sir Winston Churchill described depression as his "black dog." I prefer to visualize it as an octopus—the tentacles get into everything and affect every area of your life. The National Institute of Health gives the following information on the impact depression can have on a person's life:

> Clinical depression affects all aspects of a person's life. It impairs our ability to sleep, eat, work, and get along with others. It damages our self-esteem, self-confidence, and our ability to accomplish everyday tasks. People who are depressed find daily tasks to be a significant struggle. They tire easily, yet cannot get a good night's sleep. They

have no motivation and lose interest in activities that were once enjoyable. Depression puts a dark, gloomy cloud over how we see ourselves, the world, and our future. This cloud cannot be willed away, nor can we ignore it and have it magically disappear.

www.allaboutdepression.com

I like the above description because it's comprehensive and accurate. To give you a better idea of how depression can affect a person, I'll give some examples. The following are composites based on *many* clients I have seen over the years. The names and pertinent details are false.

Example 1 – Janet was a young college student I saw many years ago. She was suffering from acute depression. Since it was early in my career, I didn't grasp the complete severity of her condition for a while. The first time I saw her she was wearing black from head to toe and had on a large pair of dark sunglasses that hid most of her face as well as a dark hat with a large brim.

She had almost stopped functioning—she was no longer attending classes, had broken up with her boyfriend, had gained twenty pounds, was not sleeping well, had been fired from her job due to her poor performance, and was withdrawing more and more from her friends and loved ones.

She told me that depression ran in her family. Her mother had suffered from it while Janet was growing up, and an aunt had periodic bouts as well. When I asked her why she had broken up with her boyfriend (who she seemed to care about), she replied, "He's a great guy. He deserves much better than me." She applied the same logic to pulling away from her family and friends. She truly believed that no one would want to be around her for any length of time. She cried frequently and said she knew her friends were "sick of her."

She had stopped going to school because she was no longer able to concentrate and pay attention in class. When there was an assignment, she felt overwhelmed and helpless and would end up staring at the paper for hours without doing any of the required work. She said she felt like a complete failure and had "given up on life."

Example 2 – Carla was a single woman in her fifties who had been depressed most of her life. She suffered from a low level depression (dysthymia) that periodically dipped down into a major depressive episode. She told me she had been depressed since her early twenties—over thirty years!

For the most part, she was able to cope—she performed well at her job, and had good relationships with a few family members and friends. However, her depression had caused her marriage to end. She stated that her husband "couldn't put up with my moods." She was constantly exhausted (since acting "normal" required such a huge effort) and frequently felt stressed, inundated, and hopeless.

She suffered from very low self-esteem and was extremely critical of herself. She admitted to being a perfectionist and had a difficult time delegating things at work—because her coworkers didn't do things to her exacting standards. She said she would like to participate in more social activities (concerts, movies, sporting events) but didn't because by the time she made it home she was too exhausted to do anything except stare at the television.

Example 3 – Larry was a thirty-year old ex-military blue-collar worker who had suffered from depression for the last five to six years. He did fairly well in the army because he didn't have to make many decisions for himself, and he worked and lived in a very structured environment. When he left the military, his condition worsened.

He had great difficulty finding and keeping jobs since his energy and motivation were extremely low. He was very quiet and, while competent enough in his field of employment, came across as unenthusiastic and uncaring. When he did eventually get a job, he usually lost it in a few months. He was sick frequently and had trouble staying focused on the tasks he was supposed to do. His employers said he was unreliable and late or absent too much. In our sessions, I noticed he had flat affect (not much facial expression) and spoke in a monotone.

I asked him how he spent his time. He had no friends, and the only people he had regular contact with were family members. He had no hobbies or interests because "nothing seems like fun." (This is a very common symptom of depression, more commonly called adhedonia.) He was living in his parents' basement because he could no longer afford his own place.

In spite of his family's urging, Larry had quit attending church with them. He stated, "God is done with me." (I can assure you this is *never* the case!) He claimed to be "tired all the time and just a big loser." He believed he would always feel this way and had begun to seriously consider suicide.

All of the above examples illustrate very well how the dark octopus can get its tentacles into every area of a person's life. All too often depressed individuals are told to "just snap out of it" (if only it were that easy!), or "think positive thoughts." These remarks are usually made by well-meaning but ignorant individuals who have never dealt with depression personally and have no idea how it can overtake a person's life.

Most of us are aware that depression has an emotional component because we've either felt it ourselves or seen it in someone else. However, what many of us fail to realize is how depression negatively affects someone's entire being. Let's take a closer look at that dark octopus now.

How Depression Affects Your Life

I have never suffered from a major depression (for which I am extremely thankful), but I have been depressed. Most people have been unhappy at one time or another, and this is different from a major depressive disorder or episode. However, even being depressed for a short time can cause some of the symptoms we'll be looking at in this section.

During a sixteen-month period starting in October of 2010, my family experienced three deaths—my mother, my sister, and my husband. The symptoms I experienced were difficulty concentrating, sluggish thought processes, difficulty sleeping, and extreme fatigue. Usually by Wednesday I felt like I was crawling through the rest of the week. At times it felt like I was trying to move through quicksand just to get anything done. All the symptoms I experienced are common in depression.

The dark octopus of depression truly gets its tentacles into every single area of your life. Nothing remains unaffected. Your thought processes, feelings, physical well-being, and religious beliefs are all negatively impacted by this illness. These areas are affected separately but also collectively. They are all interconnected, and often when one aspect is negatively impacted, it starts off a chain reaction and ultimately, all parts of your being are disturbed. Let's look at how the emotions are influenced first.

How Depression Affects You Emotionally and Socially

Depression hugely affects the emotional and social aspects of a person's life. I often describe feeling depressed as wanting to sit in a dark room and stare at a wall. Clients have told me that this is extremely accurate. Many of them have said that even watching television is too much effort. This is where it's extremely dangerous to rely on your feelings. The feelings of a depressed individual tell them to do nothing because everything is too much work. When clients confirm that this is what they've been doing (nothing!), I ask them how long it has been going on. Typically they'll say weeks to months or even years. Now comes the important part—I ask them if sitting in a dark room staring at a wall has made them feel better. In the twenty-five-plus years that I have been counseling, I have *never* had a client say yes!

If doing nothing for a while actually caused an eventual improvement, I wouldn't be writing this book. I'd just advise my clients to wait it out a little while and keep staring at the wall; in a few weeks or months, they'd start feeling better and would be able to get on with their lives. However, that doesn't work—in this case, listening to your feelings will only get you in trouble.

Drawing on the weight loss analogy again (I know I keep using it, but it's such a good one!), overweight people wanting to lose weight can't depend on their feelings either. What they *feel* like doing is eating fried foods, sweets, processed foods, carbs, etc. I know this because I've been there for years myself. This makes you feel good on a very short-term basis but does nothing to help you lose weight. Most people who want to lose weight don't *feel* like eating healthier and exercising regularly—it's too much of a struggle. Sadly, however, I have never found another way to drop the pounds!

Depressed individuals typically find that their world becomes smaller and smaller as they are able to do less and less. This is when the darkness starts encroaching and closing in over everything. At some point, they begin to withdraw from most social interactions because talking to people is too hard. They stop participating in hobbies and recreational activities because nothing is fun anymore (this is the anhedonia—lack of pleasure and inability to feel joy—that I talked about earlier). I've had many depressed clients tell me that they used to play softball, fish, golf, eat out, go to movies, be active in church, go to family get-togethers, etc., but have dropped all those activities from their lives. They all feel like they were too much effort and aren't enjoyable anyway.

Many depressed people make some effort to appear fine for friends and coworkers and manage to get through the day *looking* all right. When they get home however, their true self comes out. They are so exhausted from the continuous effort they've made all day that they can barely talk. Because of this, their family consistently gets the short end of the stick. Usually their spouse is the most shortchanged because they will try harder for their children. I've had spouses say, "I feel like I get the crumbs that are left over."

A depressed person's body language and words (or lack of them) give off a consistent message, "Go away and quit bothering me." If this continues long enough, friends and family may start doing just that. This is not helpful either. When they're alone, depressed people usually feel scared and miserable. (My own observation—personal and professional—is that many men who are depressed come across as angry rather than scared.) So again, their feelings tell them to send everyone away so they can be left in peace, but they don't really want that, and it's not beneficial.

People with long-term depression are more likely to experience panic attacks than those without a history of depression. A panic attack is a sudden, intense fear or anxiety. The symptoms can mimic the signs of a heart attack and are often very frightening. Symptoms can include racing heart (palpitations), chest pains, dizziness, tingling or numbness in the hands and fingers, feeling sweaty or having chills, breathing difficulties, feeling a loss of control and a sense of terror, of impending doom or death. Many people experiencing a panic attack believe they are dying and rush to a hospital—only to be told their heart is fine, and they're probably having a panic attack.

As I stated previously, all areas of a person's life are affected by depression and often impact each other. The emotional facet has a tremendous influence on the mental facet as we will see next.

How Depression Affects You Mentally

People who have battled depression for a long period of time often find that it's literally hard to think straight. It can be almost impossible to accomplish anything because all the following thought functions are disturbed:

- Concentration
- Memory
- Decision making
- Thinking processes
- Organizational skills

Concentration

It's very common for a depressed individual to scan simple directions or a magazine article several times and not be able to focus on what they're reading. This can make school or work very difficult. Leisure time is also affected—following the plot of a television show or movie can be challenging—and irritating to the family or friends they're watching it with! Sometimes even participating in a chat is demanding—the thread of the discussion is dropped and lost so many times that conversational partners lose patience and give up. Typically during a counseling session with a depressed client, I have to repeat the same question several times; and while the client is talking to me, they often lose their train of thought and ask me what we were discussing.

Memory

Memory is hugely disturbed by depression. Depressed individuals forget appointments, dates, names, assignments, addresses, phone numbers, meetings, job interviews, homework, birthdays, anniversaries, etc. This can be incredibly annoying to those around them—and difficult not to take personally. I often describe depressed clients as having "holes in their memories." Clients have told me they feel like they're operating in a fog where nothing is clear—or a dream where they only see bits and pieces but never the whole picture. I had one client who told me he tried to make lists of things he was supposed to do, but he kept losing the lists! It can appear humorous to outsiders, but trying to function with an impaired memory is no joke for a depressed individual.

Not only are they very forgetful, but also frequently, the things they *do* remember are sad, gloomy, and unhappy.

This is because depression seems to pull memories in a negative direction. It makes sense. Think about a time when you were relaxed and happy with a group of loved ones. You're all feeling good and reminiscing about old times. Most of what you're remembering is positive, funny, and affectionate. The mood and atmosphere you're in influences what you remember. The same thing (in reverse) happens to unhappy people. Since they feel so down and gloomy, what they remember and focus on is unhappy, cheerless, and distressing. Often a vicious cycle of melancholy memories develops, and this doesn't help their general mood.

Decision Making

Depressed people drive themselves, and those around them, crazy with their inability to make decisions. They can agonize over the smallest detail and frequently procrastinate well past deadlines because they can't make up their minds. Since people suffering from depression typically have very black-and-white thinking, it can be painful for them to choose from several options. All the selections look bad because none of them are perfect. They will frequently put off making a decision till the last possible moment because they are afraid of making the wrong choice. They can develop what in counseling is called, "paralysis of analysis". They're totally stuck about what to do and have no idea how to fix their situation. It can be excruciating for them and distressing for loved ones to watch.

Thinking Processes

The thinking processes of depressed individuals are also affected. They are simply not as fast or sharp as normal. In fact, they're usually sluggish and painfully slow. I've seen family and friends become very impatient over how long it takes a depressed person to process through something. In sessions, I've had to bite my tongue (I tend to process very quickly!) and wait for them to think about the situation and respond. The temptation is to leap in and make the decision for them. That happens frequently but is really not helpful, understandable, but not helpful.

Organizational Skills

Because of poor concentration, memory, decision making, and thinking processes, depressed individuals are likely to be completely disorganized. Their desk at work can be piled high with papers randomly stacked everywhere; their car tends to be filled with fast-food cartons, clothes, books, and misc; their homes are often a total mess with piles of stuff in every room. In short, they're a walking disaster when it comes to organization! I'm really not a neat freak (although I do like things tidy), but I'm convinced that living in a complete mess does *not* help depression. If anything, it makes the person feel worse about their abilities and worth, and then they become even more depressed. It's what we call in counseling "a negative, downward spiral." We'll talk about how to fix this later in the book.

People who suffer from ongoing depression often see themselves as victims. Clients have told me their friends and family should make more of an effort to reach out to them. Then they admit with an embarrassed look, "But when they try, I usually don't respond." So guess what? Family and friends stop trying! Depressed individuals typically have a long list of excuses for their behavior and often truly believe none of it is their fault. Clients also tell me that they don't want to be the way they are—they sometimes barely recognize themselves. But they have no idea how to start fixing the problem, and things seem hopeless and overwhelming.

In the same way that our emotional state affects our thinking, a depressed person's thought processes have a tremendous influence on the level and type of physical activity they participate in. Let's look at the physical area next.

How Depression Affects You Physically

As I discussed when we looked at the emotional side of depression, many people suffering from this disorder begin to drop activities they used to enjoy. What I've heard over the years is that these hobbies and pastimes require too much energy and effort so the person simply quits. Often family and friends miss this warning sign because the person usually withdraws gradually, not all at once. They make excuses that seem plausible, keep missing more and more of the activity, and eventually stop participating in it altogether.

Typically the depressed person makes plans to do things (join a softball team, go to a party, clean out the garage, apply for a job, wash the car, etc.) that they have every intention of carrying out. However, once it's actually time to do them, the effort required seems overwhelming, so they either don't begin at all or stop trying very early on. Consequently, depressed individuals often have stacks of half-finished or barely started projects lying around their home and office. The sight of these uncompleted tasks actually worsens the depression. I've had clients tell me, "Whenever I see the piles of things I haven't finished, I feel like *a complete failure*." They then feel even more overwhelmed and believe it's useless to try anything.

In the United States, there is a stigma attached to mental illness. It can be seen as a personal weakness and not a true medical condition. Because of this, many people turn to substances to find relief. Abuse of drugs and alcohol can bring short-term relief but is not a true answer. Aside from this, mixing antidepressants with drugs and alcohol can have lethal results and is a very bad idea.

Depression has a negative impact on an individual's physical health. It can affect long-term sufferers in the following areas:

- Heart disease – Depressed patients with heart problems have more hospitalizations and can increase the chances of a second heart attack.
- Pain – Depression can cause pain and make existing pain worse. Depressed individuals may experience the following:
  - Headaches
  - Back pain
  - Muscle aches
  - Joint pain
  - Chest pain
  - TMJ (temporomandibular joint disorder)

- Sleep – Depression can interfere with sleep. People can have trouble falling and staying asleep or can sleep too much, usually as a way of escape.
- Sexual dysfunction – Depression can lead to sexual dysfunction including lack of sexual interest and enjoyment and difficulty attaining an erection.
- Immunity – Depression can cause systemic inflammation that affects the entire body. Infections occur more frequently in patients who suffer from symptoms of depression.
- Appetite – Depression can lead to eating more or less than usual. So weight loss, or weight gain, are common side effects.
- Chronic fatigue – People who suffer from long-term depression are more vulnerable to anything from feeling lethargic to flat-out exhaustion. Their difficulties sleeping make this area even worse.

When your emotional, mental, and physical health is negatively impacted, it can lead to a decline in your spiritual life. We'll look at that next.

How Depression Affects You Spiritually

One of the issues depressed individuals struggle with is allowing their feelings to control them. This is understandable, because their feelings are so overpowering and so overwhelmingly negative it can be difficult to function at all. But I've always believed it's risky to allow your feelings to guide your spiritual life.

I've had many depressed clients tell me over the years that they can't feel God—he appears to be absent from their lives. What I've tried to point out is that their depression doesn't allow them to feel that *anyone* loves or cares about them, and I attempt to help them find evidence disputing this. I ask if their family, coworkers, and friends are still around. Do they still express concern, come by, or try to engage you? If the answer is yes, then they probably still care about you. In the same way, just because we can't feel God, it doesn't mean he is no longer present for us.

Frequently depressed individuals experience anger toward God: "If he really loves me, why doesn't he just fix me"? This is a valid question and one asked by people suffering from other conditions as well (epilepsy, heart problems, poverty, prejudice, etc.). I'm not a minister (although there are a lot of them in my family), but here is how I understand it. We live in a fallen world. This may sound a little hollow because it's a common phrase. But we really should think about what it means. What we need to remember is the way everything we are familiar with operates (society, families, businesses, churches, schools, etc.) is *not* the way God designed it. Nothing in our world is as our Creator meant for it to be, and we are all impacted by it.

When God created our world, he set some rules in place—one of the main ones for this discussion is that we all have free will. This is the classic "good news, bad news." The good news is that we have the freedom to choose our course—to try to please God by obeying his commands and helping each other out. The bad news is that we don't do this nearly as often as we should. And God frequently allows us to suffer from the consequences of our choices. (Not only that, but also we can suffer the consequences of other people's choices as well.)

Most of the time God chooses not to interfere when we choose to sin. So he watches sadly as we lie, steal, cheat, and engage in activities that aren't good for us. Could God step in and stop things from happening? Of course he could, but usually he chooses not to. Doing so would infringe on the free will he has given us, and even if we consistently choose not to follow the rules God has set in place, he *does* follow them. So with regret and longing, he allows us to mess up our lives and try to muddle through—often only asking for his help when things are at a crisis level.

This may sound as if I'm implying that people *choose* to be depressed, and that is not the case at all. My point is that living in a fallen world has consequences. Here are some I'm aware of:

- I believe our DNA has been corrupted. Some people now have genetic tendencies toward depression, alcoholism, anxiety, bipolar, addictions, and possibly homosexuality. *God did not design us this way!*

- Due to sin in our lives, we all have a very limited understanding of God. The Living Bible puts it very well, "In the same way, we can see and understand only a little about God now, as if we were peering at his reflection in a poor mirror; but someday we are going to see him in his completeness, face to face. Now all that I know is hazy and blurred, but then I will see everything clearly, just as clearly as God sees into my heart right now" (I Cor. 13:12). Our tendency is to think God is (or should be) _____ (fill in the blank). We do our best to put him in a box with limitations we understand and can deal with. However, God doesn't fit in a box, and we will *never* fully understand him until we get to heaven. So we often become angry because God isn't

doing _____ (again, fill in the blank).
The problem is that whatever we want God
to do may be something he *never* promised us.
Many times it's not that God is at fault, it's that
our understanding of him is imperfect, and our
expectations are completely unrealistic.

- Satan is alive and well on planet Earth. I know
many people don't believe in Satan or hell,
and to be honest, I often wish I didn't either.
Unfortunately, the evidence supporting both is
too overwhelming to ignore. The Bible calls Satan
"a liar and the father of lies" (John 8:44, NIV).
Satan's ultimate purpose is simple—he wants to
separate us from God, eternally if possible. So he
will twist things, deceive us, and lead us astray;
and often he doesn't have to try too hard to do it.

So because we live in a fallen world, all we have ever
known is a corrupted and very watered-down version
of what God originally created. Things that we take for
granted as being normal are not what our creator ever
intended for them to be. I believe that God never designed
any of us to be bipolar, schizophrenic, crippled, arthritic,
blind, deaf, overweight, depressed, etc. We have those
tendencies due to sin in our world. Could God fix all
those things? Of course—in an instant (and I often wish
he would!). However, in many cases, that would involve
removing our free will, and that is something God won't
do. God wants us to obey him because we want to, as a
free choice on our part, not because we're all mindless
puppets who have no say in the matter.

There's something else that can be hard to understand, and I'll admit, I still struggle with it. I believe at times God allows us to suffer because it serves a greater purpose. Unfortunately, it can be difficult to know what that purpose is when you're in the middle of a bad situation. It can also be difficult to care about what that purpose is. All we know is that we want things to get better—*now*! Please understand. I am not saying that everyone who is suffering is doing it because God wants them to. My experience indicates that most of the time we suffer because of things we have done (or not done) or due to things others have done or not done. We can be very quick to blame God for things that, in all honesty, we brought upon ourselves. In the middle of bad situations, I have prayed many times, "Lord, if I'm still here because I need to learn or do something, please show me what it is. I'll do whatever I need to so I can get out of this situation quickly." I have prayed this very fervently and not at all irreverently.

Many Christians make the big (but understandable) mistake of telling no one about their struggles. After all, Christians aren't supposed to be depressed, right? As saved people, we should have all the answers, and life should be rosy at all times. I hate to be the bearer of sad tidings, but Christians have bad hair days, flat tires, bankruptcies, divorces, misunderstandings, and illnesses. But somewhere along the way, churchgoers have gotten the idea that life should be perfect, and we should never admit we are having any problems, especially emotional ones. So when we're in church, we all put on our little masks and never admit we are hurting and need help. This is particularly heartrending because our church should be the one place where we can be honest with each other and admit our failings.

Many depressed people quit going to church altogether, even if they were previously attending regularly. Like everything else in their lives, church attendance and participation requires too much effort. As discussed earlier, I believe their general misunderstandings about God play a large part in their decision. After all, if you believe God has abandoned you and no longer cares anything about you, why would you want to go to his house or talk to him? The sad thing is that this is probably the time we need God most. And remember, *he never leaves us*—we turn away from him.

How Your Depression Affects Your Family and Friends

What I have seen through the years, and experienced personally with Ed and my sons, is that depression is an individual condition that greatly impacts the family and beyond—friends, coworkers, and community. Let's look at the effect on family and friends first.

When long-lasting depression (major depressive disorder or dysthymia) first sets in, family and friends are usually sympathetic and understanding. They offer comfort and try to be generally helpful. If the depression is not long term and the individual begins to revert to normal, all is well. But when weeks and months pass and there is no change in the depressed person's condition (or it worsens), loved ones may become confused and worried. There are many misconceptions about depression, and one of the most prevalent is that the depressed person should just "snap out of it." If only it were that easy.

Bewilderment soon gives way to feelings of helplessness—nothing the family does seems to make things any better. There can be a sense of powerlessness and despair that can quickly lead to frustration. I'm a trained therapist, and I still found myself feeling very resentful in the early stages of Ed's depression. He had a great family and set of friends, a good job, nice house, etc., etc. Why wasn't this enough to make him happy? What more did he need?

The next stage I've seen and experienced is feelings of guilt. I found that in order to function, I had to emotionally detach myself from Ed. If I had kept that emotional connection intact, I was afraid he would pull me into the depression with him. I still don't know if it's true or not, but it's how I felt at the time. I believe this is very common because I've heard countless family members of depressed individuals tell me the same thing. Pulling away was difficult, but in the end, I chose *not* to allow Ed's depression to claim another victim.

It's also difficult to think clearly about a situation when you're in the middle of it trying your best to muddle through. All I knew was that we had two young sons and a household to run, so someone had to be functioning well. I was the emotionally strong one, so I was elected. Frequently I struggled with resentment over being the strong one. It felt like everything got dumped on me because Ed knew I could handle it. Again, I've heard others express very similar views.

Along with emotional distance, loved ones may also start keeping physical distance. Living with a depressed person is like having a big dark cloud hovering over (and inside) your entire house. Home can become a place where no one wants to be. I've had clients describe this to me exactly: "I find excuses not to go home, I hate being there." This can also intensify guilt if the depressed person is at home alone most of the time. We experienced this with Ed, and it was a lose-lose situation. We felt bad when we were at home because it was such a sad and gloomy place, and we felt guilty when we weren't there because we were avoiding Ed. At times it felt like we were abandoning him, but none of us knew what else to do. Survival mode kicks in, and you just do whatever you can to carry on.

As mentioned earlier, resentment is frequently present, along with anger. Family members resent the depressed person no longer functioning well; others have to assume their responsibilities or things are left undone. I've mentioned elsewhere that depressed individuals frequently have a victim mentality. Ed fit this description perfectly. He consistently chose *not* to do things that he knew would make him feel better and/or consistently chose to do things he knew would make him feel worse. Then he complained about how terrible his life was, how bad he felt, etc. He expected and wanted lots of sympathy and understanding and felt very ill-treated when he didn't get any. Again, I've heard this same scenario almost verbatim from family members of depressed people countless times.

I'm going to use the weight loss metaphor again because it's one I'm very familiar with. Let's say I needed to lose fifty pounds and told people this was my goal. Then I proceeded to eat lots of fatty, fried, sugary, and unhealthy foods and never exercised. That would be my choice (not a good one!), and I would have every right to do it if I wanted. What I would *not* have a right to do in this scenario is moan and complain about how I never lost weight and expect to get lots of sympathy from those around me.

When family members and friends see a depressed person sitting around day after day and making no effort to improve things (even small efforts), not only do they tend to not feel sympathetic, they frequently feel resentful and angry. Please hear me. I feel great sympathy for depressed individuals and wouldn't wish that on my worst enemy. I realize they didn't ask for the depression and often may have inherited a genetic predisposition toward it. But all that being said, the only one who can really make things better is the depressed person. It's a very hard, long, exhausting process, and if I could change it, I would. Sometimes life is just unfair, and we have no choice but to deal with it. The fact is that family and friends are much more apt to be understanding and accommodating if they see the depressed person making regular efforts to get better.

Somewhere along the way, if the depression persists over time, loved ones move into grief. No, the person may not have died (although truthfully everyone might wish they had), but the family is grieving anyway. The person they used to know is no longer there. The spouse, parent, child, or friend they loved and enjoyed being with is gone—and no one knows if they will be coming back. So there is grief for what has been lost and may never be regained. There may also be sorrow for what was hoped for and will likely never be—loss of expectations. If the depression goes on long enough, at some point the family realizes their loved one may never recover (or recover fully). All those dreams will probably never come true— no traveling, no job promotions, no new house, no shared joy over grandchildren, no more companionship, etc. This can be a time of great sadness for the family, and as a result of it, they may distance themselves even further from the depressed individual as a form of protection.

How Depression Affects Your Coworkers and Workplace

As mentioned earlier, the force of depression is felt far beyond the home. It has a profound impact in the workplace as well. Major depressive disorder is the leading cause of disability among adults ages fifteen to forty-four and affects nearly 7 percent of adults in the United States every year, according to the National Institute of Mental Health. The Depression Center of the University of Michigan notes that 15–20 percent of the workforce suffers from depression or depression-related illnesses. These cost the economy $23 billion every year in lost productivity. Most of this is due to *presenteeism*—employees show up for work but are unable to function due to depression. They may include the following:

- Miss deadlines or meetings
- Fail to return e-mails or phone calls

- Turn in substandard work

Scott Wallace, PhD, R.Psych., addresses this in his article "Depression in the Workplace" (www.healthyplace.com, Feb. 5, 2007). He notes that depression can affect an employee's productivity, judgment, ability to work with others, and overall job performance. Difficulties in concentration can lead to mistakes and/or accidents that can be expensive to correct. He notes the following signs that may indicate an employee is depressed:

- Decreased or inconsistent productivity
- Absenteeism, tardiness, or frequent absences from workstation
- Increased errors and/or diminished work quality
- Procrastination and/or missed deadlines
- Withdrawal from coworkers
- Overly sensitive and/or emotional reactions
- Decreased interest in work
- Slowed thoughts
- Difficulty learning and remembering
- Slow movement and actions
- Frequent comments about being tired all the time

It is understandable that coworkers may also become impatient and resentful if they consistently have to make extra efforts to accommodate someone who is not functioning up to par (and yes, I know they may be trying). The depressed individual, meanwhile, is between a rock and a hard place. If they don't explain their condition, coworkers may just think they are lazy and unmotivated. If they open up about their depression, they may be viewed in an unfavorable light. So often a conspiracy of silence is imposed on the family, whether they want it or not. Ed was insistent in not wanting anyone to know about his depression. Immediate family and a handful of friends knew some of what was going on. The only ones who knew the full picture were David, Josh, and me; and many times we felt very isolated because of it.

The Americans with Disabilities Act prevents employers with fifteen or more employees from discriminating against people with serious health problems (including depression), and it requires that disabled employees be accommodated. However, in order to be protected by the law, employees must disclose the nature of their disability to their employer. Often employees are afraid to report their depression to their employers because there is still a stigma surrounding depression. They may have concerns that

- they may jeopardize their job,
- they may be viewed as weak or ineffective,
- people will find out and talk about them (unfavorably).

These are all valid concerns, and I have heard depressed clients express them many times. There is another concern in using insurance for mental health. Once a person receives a diagnosis, which must be made for an insurance company to pay a claim, it can follow them around for years. I am always very cautious in what I put down as a diagnosis for that very reason. I have had clients pay in cash even when they have good mental health insurance because they don't want that type of diagnosis to be on their record (this is perfectly legal by the way).

As you can see, the economic cost of depression alone is staggering. The impact on the family and community is enormous and has far-reaching effects. Depression tends to affect people in the peak of their working years and, if left untreated, can last for decades. That may sound like an exaggeration, but I have had clients tell me they have been depressed for twenty, thirty, forty, and fifty years. It seems unbelievable that people would live with an untreated condition that long, but it happens frequently. Depression can be difficult to understand and treat because there is no one single cause. We'll look at factors that can cause and/or contribute to depression next.

Emotional Factors

One of the many puzzling aspects about depression is pinpointing the cause. A great deal of research has been done and is continuing in this area. Unfortunately, there are no quick, easy answers. When I was in school for my bachelor's degree, the big question concerning causes of many different conditions was heredity vs. environment. What we are now discovering with many ailments is that both genetics and surroundings play a part. Let's look at emotional/social issues that cause and contribute to depression first.

1. One characteristic I have noted frequently in depressed individuals is *perfectionism*. They expect and want everything to be perfect, and when that doesn't happen, they feel like failures. The problem is that their standards are so unrealistically high, no one can reach them. Often, in their eyes, this just confirms how terrible life is.

They can hold impossibly high expectations for others as well, and this can be dangerous. I have heard family members of depressed individuals say something like the following *many* times: "Nothing I do is ever good enough for Mom, so after a while, I just quit trying." If your loved ones know there is no pleasing you, they may stop making any effort to do so and distance themselves further as a form of self-protection.

2. *Lack of flexibility* – Depressed individuals typically do *not* roll well with the punches. If things don't go according to their plan, life is not good. Ed's life was full of "shoulds" and "ought tos." I often thought he had some preset agenda he was determined to follow come heck or high water. He did *not* like surprises, and the slightest deviation in routine could throw him into a tailspin. He had a terrible time making decisions quickly, especially in response to a sudden change of some kind. The boys learned, very early on, to come to me if they needed a speedy verdict. Ed (and many other depressed individuals I have observed) seemed to have a set of very black-and-white rules that dominated his life. Often these rules made sense to no one except him, and he became very upset when they weren't followed scrupulously.

I often describe depressed people as *being controlled by their feelings*—they feel bad, therefore life is bad. The problem with this is it assumes the way they feel is actually reflective of reality when often this is not the case. This is easy to understand because we all do it to some extent. Let's say there is an accident on the way to work that causes you to be late, several important reports are accidently deleted from your computer, and you get a call from your son's school saying he is running a fever and asking you to come get him—all before 10:00 a.m. At this point you are feeling stressed, overwhelmed, and negative. But is your whole life stressed, overwhelming, and negative? Not really, and if you don't allow yourself to be controlled by your feelings, you will know this because everything that happened is fixable. You tell yourself that you can stay a little later at work the next day to make up for being late. While you are home with your sick child, you can redo the reports and e-mail them into work, and children get sick frequently but it's usually not serious. Your son will probably be better tomorrow. You recognize that all these are temporary setbacks that can be overcome.

The depressed person, on the other hand, will give herself the following messages. "I can't believe I was late today—my boss gave me such a dirty look that I know he wants to fire me. And what happened to those reports? I can't believe I was stupid enough to lose them—I'll never be able to do them over! And now Johnnie is sick—he's probably coming down with pneumonia, and I'll have to take him to the hospital. My life is such a mess—I just can't cope. I think everyone would be better off if I were dead." As you can see, a depressed person's feelings can color their entire world in very dark, dismal, and gloomy shades.

3. *Egocentrism* is another trait I have observed in depressed individuals. Frequently they don't mean to be this way, but over time a preoccupation with their condition can develop and may give them the assumption that life revolves around them—their needs, problems, and condition. Many times it's as if they have tunnel vision, and their depression blinds them to everyone but themselves. I know from experience and observation that this is *not* an enjoyable characteristic for the rest of the family to live with. I often thought (but never dared say out loud!) that while Ed was not a selfish person, he *was* an extremely self-centered one. He frequently became frustrated when the rest of us didn't treat his needs as paramount or allow his depression to excuse him from taking care of his responsibilities. From what I have seen and heard, this appears to be pretty typical for depressed individuals.

4. Other factors that can cause depression are *stressful and/or traumatic life events*, especially ones happening at an early age. These can include things like

   - parents divorcing;
   - moving to another city;
   - being in a bad car wreck;
   - surviving a bad fire, earthquake, tornado, or natural disaster;
   - sexual trauma;

- severe bullying;
- death of a loved one (including a pet).

According to the Association for Psychological Science (APS), it appears that stressful events (such as those listed above), particularly experienced early in life, cause changes in the central nervous system that result in physical and behavioral changes. Early-life stress appears to radically alter neurobiological systems involved in the pathophysiology of depression. In other words, suffering stress *early* in life makes us more vulnerable to stress *later* in life (July/August, 2010, "Childhood Trauma & Depression," *Observer* Vol. 23, No. 6). I believe this often happens because parents underestimate the impact traumatic events have on children. Often children don't talk much about what happened to them—sometimes they don't have the verbal skills to do so. So parents assume things are fine and don't get their children the help they need. Years later these now-grown individuals may develop depression, anxiety, and a host of other emotional and physical problems.

5. One of the things I have seen frequently over the years is that *even the healthiest person can become depressed if several bad things happen in a short period of time.* Some people have a good amount of what in psychology we call "hardiness". This is a characteristic that allows a person to accept changes, challenges, and difficulties in life with good humor and an even temper. These people practice behaviors that tend to prevent them from

getting sick. This is a desirable character trait, and these people are less likely to develop depression. However, even the hardiest individual can become depressed if numerous bad things happen in a short enough time. I've had clients who normally coped very well with life until they lost their job, found out they had cancer, discovered their spouse was cheating on them, and totaled their car—all within two weeks. These are sometimes called *compounded losses.*

Remember Job in the Bible? He lost all his animals (which represented a good part of his wealth), most of his servants, and all ten of his children—in the same day! It's understandable that his wife urged him to "curse God and die." My point here is that, although some people are less prone to depression than others, anyone can become depressed in the right (or wrong) circumstances. No one is completely immune.

6. If you have been depressed for a long time, you have probably developed *a sense of hopelessness* (you believe the depression will never get better) and *helplessness* (you believe nothing you do will make things any better).

Often depressed individuals develop a sense of learned helplessness. This is a condition first observed by Martin Seligman in animal experiments he was conducting in the mid-sixties at the University of Pennsylvania. He and his colleagues accidently discovered that conditioning dogs led to outcomes that opposed B. F. Skinner's behaviorism (a leading psychological theory at the time).

In the learned helplessness experiment, an animal was repeatedly hurt by an adverse stimulus (usually a small electrical shock) from which there was no escape. Eventually the animal stopped trying to avoid the pain and behaved as if it was helpless to change the situation. In time, opportunities to escape were given, but by then, the animal's learned helplessness prevented them from taking any action. The animals became very stoical and put up with the discomfort, making no attempt to escape the adverse stimulus, even when a way out was available.

Seligman is the founder of the *positive psychology* movement (the scientific study of the strengths and virtues that enable individuals and communities to thrive) and has written several excellent books. If you are a depressed person (or have a loved one who suffers this condition), I recommend *Learned Helplessness*. I have found it very helpful in understanding the thinking processes of a depressed person.

Ed fit the learned helplessness description perfectly. I was puzzled by his behavior for years. We would discuss things he could do to make things better, he would agree and then would never do them. After reading several of Seligman's books, I realized Ed was convinced nothing he could do would ever make things better, so why bother trying. This mentality was both frustrating and incomprehensible to me because I strongly believe that I *can* make a difference in my circumstances, and I'm from the try-try-and-try-again school of thought. Ed and I were so far apart in our outlooks on life that at times it was as if we were speaking completely different languages. I realize now that Ed often felt defeated before he even started something.

When I look at his behavior from a learned helplessness perspective, it makes more sense. Let's say a new boss took me to the roof of a twelve-story building and told me my job was to figure out how to fly. She encouraged me to flap my arms really hard and think light thoughts and, when I was ready, to jump off the building. I can say with a great deal of assurance that, in spite of her confidence in my abilities, I would *never* believe I could fly. Because of that, would I waste any time flapping my arms on the rooftop? Not at all. I would be busy looking for a new job! In this situation, *not* trying is the logical choice and the smart thing to do. Why waste time and energy in an impossible situation?

Although saving my strength would be the appropriate response in the above scenario, this is usually not the case for a depressed individual. I am clearly not capable of flying, but depressed people *are* capable of many of the following:

- Going for a job interview
- Cleaning out the garage
- Attending a family function
- Walking the dog
- Making a presentation at work
- Cooking a meal

- Putting gas in the car
- Returning library books
- Going to a church service

Often the lack of ability is in the depressed individual's mind. They believe they are incapable of performing the task (usually because they can't do it perfectly!), so they don't even make the attempt. Our thoughts/beliefs truly affect our feelings and our actions. Let's look at mental factors that can cause or contribute to depression next.

Mental Factors

People who are depressed tend to view everyone and everything around them through their depression, as if they are wearing a pair of dark glasses that affect their perceptions. So everything is experienced in a negative, sad, and undesirable way. Consequently, the person begins to think the world is a negative, sad, and undesirable place. Here are some examples of harmful thinking that can provoke and lead to depression.

1. *Unrealistic expectations* – these go hand in hand with perfectionism.

   As mentioned before, depressed individuals often have such irrationally high standards that no one can reach them. Let me clarify. There's nothing wrong with high standards, but they need to be reasonably attainable. If not, they just set us up for frustration. I'll give an example.

Let's say I want to become healthier. I've gone to the doctor, and she says I need to lose fifty pounds. My blood pressure is high, and I could easily develop diabetes since it runs in my family. So I decide (reluctantly) that I need to start eating healthier and working out. I haven't exercised in years, but I was on the track team in high school, so I resolve to start running again. The first day I elect to go on a five-mile run (I want to get in shape quickly). You can imagine the rest. I am only able to run about half the distance, I develop shin splints and blisters and feel terrible the next day—so bad, in fact, that I decide running is a terrible idea, and I resolve never to do it again.

Is running a bad activity? Of course not, but running five miles the first time is simply too much. I've set an unrealistically high (and not very smart!) goal for myself that I'm not going to be able to attain. So I get angry and discouraged, and I quit. This whole scenario could have been avoided if I had set a more reasonable goal— maybe trying for one mile a day, three times a week to start out.

2. *Black-and-white thinking* – In the depressed person's world, things are either perfect or horrible. There is very little middle ground. Since things are seldom perfect, they are usually horrible. This is a formula for unhappiness when you think about it. How often are things perfect? Not very often. Let's be generous and say 10 percent of the time. That means that a person with these thought

processes is going to be miserable 90 percent of the time. Now that's depressing!

This type of thinking is also known as the *false dilemma*. Only two alternatives are presented when, in fact, there may be more options present. This mentality doesn't allow any compromise and refuses to consider alternative solutions. It's very limited in its outlook and is often not logical. The depressed person frequently operates as if they have blinders on and is limited by their "either/or" mentality. I've seen this in many depressed individuals. They tell their loved ones (either openly or implicitly), "You're either for me or against me." Getting them to even consider other options than the ones they are personally aware of can be challenging.

3. *A desire to be in control* – Of everything. Depressed individuals often believe things need to be done a certain way (their way!). When this doesn't happen, they may feel extreme anxiety, which usually leads to a sense of failure and depression. At times, however, this quality can go the other way. Some depressed people believe they have no control over anything and have quit trying. This relates back to learned helplessness, which I discussed earlier.

I've often thought that a high desire for control is simply arrogance. It's also extremely futile. How much power do we have over events anyway? Not nearly as much as we sometimes think or would like to have. A few years ago, I heard a therapist talk about a group he had been running. One participant routinely took responsibility for things that were not her fault. Finally, the therapist had her go around to everyone in the group and apologize for everything that was wrong in their lives—because it was all her fault! About the time she reached the third person, she began to realize the ridiculousness of her belief. The other group members did as well. They were laughing and responding with, "I've been looking for you a long time—where have you been?" Trust me. Being responsible for ourselves is more than enough.

4. Depressed people tend to have lots of *shoulds* and *rules for how things need to be done.* It's as if they have a tiny rule keeper in their head constantly telling them they're not measuring up. Frequently these rules make no sense and even seem ridiculous. Once, early in our marriage, we were going to a friend's house for a cookout. Ed demanded that we both dress up—a lot. I explained several times that backyard cookouts were typically casual. He kept insisting that *they* said it was better to be more formal. I finally asked him who *they* were. He got angry and never answered. We went to the cookout and were the best-dressed couple present! He had on slacks and a nice shirt while I was wearing a dress—everyone else wore shorts, T-shirts, and sandals. I see now that one of Ed's rules was that it's better to be overdressed than casual, even if it's inappropriate.

5. Another behavior that can contribute to depression is *overgeneralizing,* basing your thoughts and feelings on one experience and generalizing it to everything else and expecting it to be true forever. Here's an example. Sarah has been invited to her friend LuAnn's house for a sleepover. Several other girls who attended another school are also present and, without meaning to, made Sarah feel excluded. She has a terrible time at the sleepover and goes home determined never to go to another one (because sleepovers are horrible experiences), is convinced that all the girls there disliked her and believes that *everyone* would *always* dislike her— forever! This is the type of thinking that many depressed individuals experience on a regular basis. You can probably see why this mentality can lead to depression.

6. Many chronically depressed people have a *negative mental filter*—everything is viewed through "dark glasses," so it all appears to be bad. What always amazed me about Ed is how he could totally ignore all the good, positive things and immediately zoom in on the bad ones. This is very typical for depressed individuals. Twenty good things can happen with one bad one, guess what they focus on? They completely disregard 95 percent of what has happened and focus on the 5 percent that was less than ideal.

7. Something that goes along with the negative mental filter is *discounting positive experiences.* This involves coming up with reasons why the

good experiences aren't really valid and don't count. I have seen this over and over in depressed individuals. I'll give an example. Frank has made a presentation at work that overall went very well. His coworkers made several appreciative comments, and his boss told him he had done an excellent job. However, the general manager was in attendance and walked out during the presentation—to take a phone call. All Frank remembers is the manager was so bored during his report that he left. When Frank's secretary reminds him of the positive comments others made, he replies, "They were just being nice, they didn't really mean it." He totally invalidates everything positive and zeroes in on the one negative (which was really only negative in his mind!). This probably sounds somewhat humorous, but I can assure you it happens with great regularity in depressed individuals' lives, and this trait greatly contributes to a negative mood.

8. Something else depressed people are very good (or very bad!) at is *jumping to conclusions,* making negative interpretations with little or no actual evidence. These people automatically assume the worst possible outcome for situations. This is related to *catastrophizing,* and Ed was a genius at it! In the beginning of our relationship, I was baffled by his constant assumptions of disaster. He often said he was a master of making a mountain out of a molehill, and he was right! In these people's minds, the boss asking them to come into his office is a sure sign they are going to be fired,

or a pain in the abdomen is instantly interpreted as a malignant cancer tumor. (As you may have guessed, hypochondriacs frequently catastrophize as well).

9. Depressed individuals habitually believe things will go wrong, which can lead to what is called a *self-fulfilling prophecy*. This is a prediction that causes itself to come true. An example would be—Jane is dreading going to her friend Tara's birthday party. Her thinking goes something like this: "I'm so bad at meeting new people. I never know what to say to them, and people always think I'm boring. I know when I get to the party no one will want to talk to me, and I'll have a rotten time." Guess what happened at the party? You got it! She looked so uncomfortable and awkward that very few people made an effort to talk to her. When they did, her body language and stilted conversation made it very clear that she had nothing to say, so the partygoers quickly left her alone. Jane's *beliefs* (or thoughts) made her prediction come true. This happens to depressed individuals all the time!

10. Something else common in depressed people's lives is illustrated in several of the preceding examples: *labeling and name calling*. This is beating yourself up because of perceived shortcomings and labeling yourself in negative ways. The depressed clients I have seen over the years have told me this is a huge issue with them. They believe they are incompetent, clumsy, unlovable, friendless, dull,

stupid, unworthy, unwanted, powerless, failures, weak, rejected, and victims. Not only do they believe this about themselves, they tell themselves these things—*all the time!* They have a litany of misery playing constantly in their heads. It's enough to make anyone depressed.

One of the interesting things about depression is what we call the *mind-body connection.* This means that what we think, believe, and feel can positively or negatively affect our biological functioning. In other words, our minds can affect how healthy our bodies are! Let's look now at some of the physical factors that cause and/or contribute to depression.

Physical Factors

1. It's easy to understand how the first physical factor can lead to depression—*severe or chronic illness*—especially an illness that starts in early childhood. Most children don't enjoy being different; they just want to fit in with their friends. So to be sidelined from normal activities due to acute asthma can be notably difficult to take. This can be even more challenging if the child has healthy siblings who are participating in sports, scouting, sleepovers, etc. (As a side note, this can be problematic for the healthy sibling as well. I've talked to many grown family members who still struggle with resentment. They know their sibling was sick, but it was tough to see them getting all of their parent's attention).

   An illness that strikes in adulthood can also be taxing, especially if it goes on for a long period of time. I've never met anyone who enjoys being sick. Most of us want to get well quickly and get back to normal. If cancer, lupus, arthritis, etc., make this impossible, it's easy to fall into a depression. Even something relatively minor, like having a leg in a cast for several months, can be trying. Things that keep us from our normal activities and make life more difficult can drain us of energy and optimism—and can easily lead to dejection, feeling sorry for ourselves, and sadness.

2. Something else that can cause depression is *side effects of medications*. It's a good idea to read about any new prescriptions carefully, especially possible side effects. If you have newly become depressed and have recently started taking a different medicine, call your doctor and let him or her know. There may be another drug available that will treat your symptoms without leading to feelings of sadness. Also be very careful of what you are taking in combination with your prescriptions. Some drugs do not combine well with certain over-the-counter medications or even some foods. If you have a question, check with your pharmacist or doctor.

3. A more serious issue that often leads to depression is *prolonged drug* or *alcohol use*. Some drugs affect brain functioning and lead straight to depression. At first glance, this may not appear to be the case. Cocaine, for example, initially elevates moods. However, when the high wears off, users frequently fall into a deep depression.

Often people who are depressed will use drugs or alcohol to self-medicate, in hopes of feeling better. The irony here is that alcohol is actually a depressant, so what usually happens is that the depression gets worse!

4. There are also several *biological factors* related to depression. I'll list some here.

- *Gender* – Women are twice as likely as men to be depressed.

- *Age* – The elderly are more likely to be depressed, especially over the age of sixty-five.

- *Thyroid disease* – Both hypo and hyperthyroidism have been linked to depression.

- *Genetics* – If you have a relative who suffers from clinical depression, you have a greater chance of developing it yourself. Depression tends to run in families, but researchers aren't sure why.

- *Previous episode* – If you have had a prior episode of depression, you are likely to have another one.

- *Sleep disturbances* – If you chronically do not get enough sleep, you are at risk for depression. According to *Psychology Today*, at least 80 percent of depressed people experience insomnia, while another 15 percent of depressed individuals sleep excessively. But insomnia may be more than just a symptom of depression; it may actually unleash the mood disorder. Sleep researcher Michael Perlis, PhD, has conducted longitudinal studies that show insomnia appears to precede episodes of depression by about five weeks. (July 2003, "Bedfellows: Insomnia and Depression." *Psychology Today*).

- *Chronic pain* – According to WebMD (depression and chronic pain), depression in patients with chronic pain frequently goes undiagnosed and, therefore, often goes untreated. During doctor visits, pain symptoms and complaints are the focus of discussion. As a result, the depression continues and can make the pain worse. Individuals with chronic pain tend to feel constantly tense and stressed. Over time, the constant stress can result in different emotional problems associated with depression, such as anger, fatigue, irritability, confused thinking, and social isolation.

5. A somewhat surprising point is the fact that *city dwellers* have a 39 percent higher risk for mood disorders than people living in the country. A 2011 study in the journal *Nature* offers a possible explanation for this trend: urbanites have more activity in the part of the brain that regulates stress. And higher levels of stress can lead to depression.

6. Something I discovered while researching this book was new for me—*internet addiction* may be associated with depression, particularly for preteens and teens. These individuals may not do well in face-to-face interactions and can have few friends. They may also have unrealistic

expectations of the world in general. Again, this area is very new, and more research needs to be done.

As you can see, various physical conditions can impact and/or cause depression. But there is one more area involved—the spiritual side. Let's look at that now.

Spiritual Factors

Often people who are depressed struggle spiritually. When overwhelming darkness is all you see, it can be easy to believe God has abandoned you. Sadly, this struggle can be made even worse because of the mistaken belief many Christians have—that if you are living a godly life, you won't struggle with emotional disorders. So depressed Christians are really in a bind. They wonder what they're doing wrong (because as Christians they shouldn't even *be* depressed), and they're afraid to ask for help because then everyone will be aware of their situation.

1. Over the years, I've known many believing clients who told me they worked very hard to keep their depression a *secret* in their church. They were afraid to let anyone know because of what others might think of them. Ed was a prime example of this. David, Josh, and I knew more about his

situation than anyone else because we lived with him. However, I believed there were many people who might have been able to help Ed if he would have opened up more. He was adamant in his refusal, however, and he would not allow us to tell anyone either.

This is very typical, and it puts the family between a rock and a hard place. I handled this by careful thought and prayer over time. I finally decided that since I was living with Ed and his depression, I needed prayer and support, and I wasn't going to get any if I didn't ask. So I was selective in who I confided in, but I eventually had a small network of family and friends who were aware of Ed's condition and who were faithful in praying for all four of us.

2. I understood Ed's desire to keep his depression a secret. There is still a stigma attached to mental health issues, and it is often evident in churches. However, I also believed some of his desire not to tell anyone came from *spiritual pride*. None of us like to reveal our weaknesses and have people see our flaws. Churches can be very bad about everyone wearing their "Sunday face" and acting as if everything is fine, even when they're falling apart. This is especially sad because the church should be the place where we can truly be ourselves and know that we'll be loved and accepted as we are. The reality, however, is that this doesn't always happen.

3. Any type of *traumatic loss*, especially early in life, can cause a person to believe God no longer cares about them and can set the stage for depression. The loss can be anything, some I have already mentioned, but I'll list them again. Parents' divorce, death (especially of a close family member), a move to another city, home destroyed in a fire, earthquake or tornado, a chronic illness experienced early in life, or a parent's addiction can all cause anger and resentment toward God. And if we are angry at God, we typically pull away and want nothing to do with him.

4. A very difficult type of loss to come to terms with is *early physical, sexual, or emotional abuse*. This type of experience can make it tough to believe in the concept of a loving and protective god. I had a client years ago who asked, "If God is all-powerful, why didn't he stop my father from beating and abusing me?" A fair question and a difficult one to answer, but I'll do my best.

As I mentioned before, we live in a fallen world. When God created the world and all that is in it (including us), he set some rules in place. When we follow those rules, things go well. When we don't, however, we, and those around us, suffer the consequences. Let me give an example. Nathan and Ben are six- and eight-year-old brothers. They're home on a Saturday, and their parents have some financial matters to take care of, so after breakfast, they tell the boys to go outside and play in the backyard. There is a swing set, sandbox, and lots of toys for them to enjoy. There is also a very large tree on one side of the yard that the boys like to climb. However, because it's so tall, the rule is that the boys aren't allowed to climb it unless a parent is present.

The parents remind the boys of the tree rule and send them outside. Things go well for the first hour or so, and then Ben gets bored and begins looking for something else to do. Nathan is tired, so he sits under the tree with some toys and plays quietly. After a while, Nathan falls asleep, and Ben decides to climb the tree. He thinks he hears some of his friends in a neighboring yard but can't see over the fence to know for sure. He remembers he is not supposed to climb the tree unless one of his parents is present but decides it won't hurt just this once. He will climb up quickly, just high enough to see over the fence, and then will get right down. Nathan is sleeping, and his parents are in the house—no one will ever know.

Ben starts climbing quietly and is soon able to see over the fence. Sure enough, some of his friends are a few houses over. He begins to descend hurriedly, and disaster strikes. He slips and falls out of the tree, screaming loudly all the way down. His parents rush out of the house and realize Ben probably has a broken leg. But that's not all. Ben has fallen on top of Nathan—and Nathan has a broken arm, a broken leg, and some cracked ribs.

What did Nathan do to deserve the broken limbs he received? Nothing! He was obeying his parents and minding his own business. He suffered the consequences of Ben's refusal to follow their parent's rules, rules that were in place to protect the boys and avoid just such a situation. This is exactly what can happen to us when we, or others, choose to disobey God's rules. We can get hurt, and often, we hurt those around us.

Please believe me when I say that God is not indifferent to human suffering, especially when innocents suffer at the hand of others. God takes this very seriously. The following scriptures both record Jesus's warning in this area:

> But if anyone causes one of these little ones who trusts in me to lose faith, it would be better for that person to be thrown into the sea with a large millstone tied around the neck.
>
> Mark 9:42 (NLT)

> One day Jesus said to his disciples, "There will always be temptations to sin, but how terrible it will be for the person who does the tempting. It would be better to be thrown into the sea with a large millstone tied around the neck than to face the punishment in store for harming one of these little ones."
>
> Luke 17:1–2 (NLT)

If you are dealing with past physical, emotional, or sexual abuse that has led you to depression, please do not make the mistake of believing that God was unconcerned about what happened to you. When you were being hurt, especially if it was done by someone who should have been protecting you, know that God was grieving for you—in the same way he grieved for his son when he was betrayed, tortured, and killed.

We all have a tendency to blame God for the bad things that happen to us when many of them were *not* caused by God at all. Many bad things occur because of choices we and others make, but God makes a handy target. How often do we give him credit for all the good things in our lives? My point is we shouldn't be so quick to assume that God causes negative events and is looking for ways to make us suffer. We do plenty, all on our own, to cause most of the suffering in our lives without God's help!

I hope that looking at things that can cause or contribute to depression has given you a better understanding of how depression occurs. Now let's look at what can be done to make things better.

Things That Can Help

At this point in the book, you've probably recognized yourself (or someone else you know) through the symptoms I've outlined. And now you're asking, "What's next? I've confirmed that I'm depressed, and I agree that it affects pretty much every aspect of my life, so what do I do about it? Am I stuck like this forever? Is there any hope of things getting better?"

Yes, there is hope, and *no*, you don't have to be depressed forever. Change is possible, but you will have to work at it—in three different ways:

- *Intensely* – Change is tough and is not for wimps.
- *Consistently* – Doing something differently once or twice isn't going to be enough.
- *Over time* – As much as we'd all like to get better *yesterday*, it's not going to happen overnight.

Getting better is very possible, but there's no point in deceiving you. It can be a difficult, uphill, drawn-out battle. And as tired of the struggle as you will get, you're the only one who can do it. So add *lonely* into the description of the struggle.

I've never dealt personally with a major emotional disorder, but trying to overcome depression is, in many ways, like trying to lose weight—and I'm an expert at that! Let me illustrate. Suppose I needed to lose one hundred pounds. There are several ways I could approach the situation.

I could get totally defeated before I even began. "One hundred pounds!" I could say. "That's a huge amount (no pun intended!). I'll never be able to do it. I just don't have that kind of willpower. It's completely impossible, so I guess I'll just have to get used to being fat." I call this the "why even bother" approach.

Next, I could be very doubtful about my ability to succeed but could start trying (reluctantly) to eat better and exercise more. With this kind of mentality, I might eat healthier and go to the gym for a week or two, but when I weighed at the end of two weeks and saw that I'd only lost five pounds, I would be completely discouraged. The results on the scale would confirm what I already knew—there's no way I can lose one hundred pounds! So I would quit trying and go get some ice cream (might as well be somewhat happy in my misery!). I call this the half-hearted approach.

A lot of people trying to lose weight never make it past the above two methods. And I have to confess, I've been in both camps many times in my life. But there is a third alternative.

I could look at where I am and where I want to be (one hundred pounds lighter). I could acknowledge that it's a big goal but also that it's one I'm capable of reaching. "After all," I could say, "I've done big projects before. I remodeled my house, and it took eight months. I landscaped my yard. It was bare dirt when I started, and it took me over a year to totally finish it, but it looks great now"!

So before I even started, I would give myself realistic messages like the following:

- I'm not going to lose all the weight quickly. It may take me over a year, but that's okay. By this time next year, think how much better I'll look and feel!
- I don't have to eat or exercise perfectly all the time to get the results I want. If I cheat on my eating or skip working out now and then, it won't make that much difference as long as I get right back on my weight loss program the next day.
- I'm not going to eat the same food all the time. That gets boring, and then I'm more likely to cheat. I'll have more than just salads and tuna. I'll try new foods and new ways of cooking on a regular basis. Some foods I won't like, but others I will.
- I also won't exercise the same way all the time. I'll do a variety of activities to use different muscle groups and to add fun to my workouts.
- I won't compare myself to others because it makes me feel bad about myself. My best friend always loses weight faster than I do (and it's really unfair!), but I'm not her. I'm me, and I'm going to

concentrate on finding weight loss routines that work for me!

- I will probably get tired of eating right and working out—after all, a year is a long time. So to stay motivated, I'll give myself rewards along the way. I'll come with something like this:
    - I'll download a new book for every five pounds I lose.
    - If I finish a 5K run, I'll get a new pair of shoes.
    - On weeks I follow my eating and exercising plan about 85 percent of the time, I'll go to a movie (and take my own nonfattening snack!).
    - When I reach half my goal weight, I'll buy some new clothes.

Hopefully, you get the idea. I call this the "realistically planning for success" approach. This is the approach you'll need to overcome depression. It will be hard, time consuming, and a lot of work, but it can be done. Let's look at how to accomplish it.

Don't Trust Your Feelings

A s I go through this book, I'll explain new material, give a goal to strive for, and then discuss ways to help you reach that goal (not always in that order). So here is your first goal for the emotional/social area:

Goal no. 1 – Don't follow your feelings.

To a certain extent, we all have a tendency to do what we feel, but this can be deadly for people battling long-term depression. I've seen this with Ed and my clients over and over—their feelings tell them to do *nothing*. It's understandable because they have no energy, no motivation, and no excitement about anything. So they have no desire to do any of the following:

- Go to work
- Talk to family or friends
- Exercise

- Get outside
- Work on any hobbies
- Go to a movie
- Go to church
- Clean up their living space

Nothing sounds worth doing, mainly because everything seems to require so much effort. Remember, depression saps you of all the good things in your life and just leaves the bad. So when the depressed person thinks about actually doing something—say going out for a meal with friends—they may initially have a glimmer of interest. However, it quickly gets smothered when they think about all they will need to do in order to go out for that meal—take a shower, change clothes, drive themselves to the restaurant, decide what they want to eat, and carry on a conversation for a couple of hours. It can feel overwhelming, so they typically give in to their feelings and just stay home.

I tell depressed clients frequently—your feelings are *not* a reliable guide. Here are a couple of tools to help you not be controlled by your emotions.

1 – Repeat this mantra, *"I don't have like it, I just have to do it."* This is something I came up with years ago in regard to exercising (I'll talk more about this in the next section). When you think about it, it makes sense. There are many things in life we don't feel like doing, but we have to do them anyway. I'll give some examples:

- Cutting the grass
- Flossing our teeth
- Cooking dinner

- Going to our child's sporting event (especially when we're tired!)
- Walking the dog
- Going to work
- Paying bills

If we were totally guided by our feelings, many of the above things (and a host of others) would never get done. Taking care of our responsibilities, whether we feel like it or not, is one of the defining characteristics of adulthood. I've never met anyone, no matter how wealthy, who has been able to do only what they feel like doing. Life simply doesn't work that way. So remind yourself that it's okay not to enjoy whatever you need to do—just do it anyway!

2 – Next helpful hint: Follow a time-honored, profound psychological principle I have shared with many clients. *Fake it till you make it.* This sounds corny, but it actually works. If you want to become a certain type of person (an athlete, for example), figure out what an athlete would be doing, and go do it! The reason this works is because of another profound little truism—*feelings follow actions.*

If you *act* a certain way long enough, eventually it won't be just a pretense—you will become the person you've been acting like. I do a fair amount of relationship counseling and get the following question pretty regularly, "What do I do if I no longer love my spouse?" Providing the client wants to stay in the marriage, the answer is pretty simple. Figure out what you would be doing if you *did* love that person and go do it.

I discovered the truth of this in college (just a few years ago!) when I worked in a day care center at a local church. I had about fifteen five-year-olds in my class, and most of them were pretty sweet and lovable. Then there was Daniel Johnson (not his real name). To say Daniel was strong-willed was putting it mildly. This was a kid who was willing to knock everyone out of the way to get what he wanted. He also wasn't very physically attractive. His mom was a single parent who worked full-time and didn't have much energy for Daniel and his siblings, so they frequently showed up in ragged clothing with runny noses and dirty faces. I'll be honest. I didn't really like Daniel at first and had a hard time being nice to him.

But God began convicting me for my attitude, so I started praying about how I could love Daniel. And trust me, my feelings were pretty far from affectionate. I didn't see how I could ever do more than tolerate him. So I asked myself what I would be doing if I loved Daniel, and slowly I started doing little things for him. I brought a comb and a washrag to the day care center that I used to try and make him a little more presentable. I got a book and sat down and read to him—to his complete amazement (sadly, I don't think anyone had ever done that before). I made a point of praising him when he did something even halfway well. The more I did, the easier it became, and after a while, I didn't have to wrack my brain to figure out what I could do to express love to Daniel—because I truly loved him! My feelings had caught up with my actions, and my heart had been changed.

I've always remembered that example and have used it often when I'm trying to alter something in my life, especially a feeling. So when I'm trying to be more physically active and lose weight, I'll ask myself, "What would I be doing right now if I felt like an energetic person?" (Hint: The answer is *not* lying on the couch!) I'll figure out what it would be, and off I go—to take a walk, ride my bike, go for a run, pull out an exercise DVD, etc. So if you're having trouble overcoming depression, a very easy technique is to ask yourself, "If I were feeling happy and cheerful right now, what would I be doing?" The answer might be

- baking a cake for my child's third grade class,
- cleaning out my car,
- finishing up my presentation for work,
- inviting my friends over to my house for dinner,
- planning a weekend getaway with my spouse,
- taking my family for a bike ride.

The possibilities are endless, but you'll notice that sitting and staring at a wall is *not* on the list. You'll also notice that the question "Do I feel like doing this?" is not asked. In this instance, feelings are unimportant because they will consistently send you astray. So (in this context) learn to ignore your feelings. Trust your thoughts more than your emotions. I also realize this is easier said than done. You may have been depressed for so long that you honestly have no idea what non-depressed people do. Again, there's an easy fix for this. Think of a couple of happy people you know and watch what they do. Better yet, ask them how they spend their time. Tell them that you're looking for some new hobbies and you're canvassing people to see what sounds good.

Start off slowly and try a few new things. The important thing here is to shake things up a bit. So don't worry if you really don't love the first new thing you try. Keep going and keep trying new activities. Frankly, you might not love any of them, so try to find ones that you don't hate and can at least tolerate. Sometimes you'll enjoy an activity more after you've done it a few times and you're more familiar with it.

Mix It Up

T he preceding section leads nicely into the next goal:

Goal no. 2–Try something new.

We are all creatures of habit, and we gravitate toward the familiar. Familiar can equal comfortable, which, to a degree, we all enjoy. This explains why we all tend to have routines we follow. There's nothing wrong with routines—believe me I have plenty of my own. They make life easier and more predictable. The problem is that too many routines can also make life dull and boring, which can exacerbate depression.

I know this goal can be difficult for many chronically depressed people. I've had clients say, "I'm barely crawling along, where am I going to get the energy to even *think* of something new to try, let alone do it?" I understand that this can be difficult and, at times, even overpowering. But try this in small steps. You don't have to run a marathon right at the beginning.

Pick something that's a variation of an activity you're already doing so you don't have to start completely from scratch. I'll give some examples below.

- Instead of eating lunch at the same restaurant during your workday, ask coworkers where they go and resolve to try one new restaurant a week. The rest of the week you can go to your regular place.
- Insert one or two new things into your regular weekend routine—no need to change everything you usually do.
- Take a class from a community college on a subject that you know a little about and are already interested in—photography, cooking, fashion, scrapbooking, etc.
- If you have trouble finding time and energy to exercise, try working out a little in the evenings while you watch TV. You can still see your favorite programs while walking on a treadmill or jumping on a rebounder. (I do both of these almost daily.)
- Do you eat the same meals on a regular basis? Don't feel bad because most of us do. Resolve to try one new food a week—either at a restaurant or cooked at home. As you find new things, you like you can incorporate them into your mealtimes.

Hopefully this makes sense, and you get the picture. Things that are new keep us fresh and more interested, but there's no need to go overboard. You don't have to change everything in your life overnight. Take it in small steps and go slow. Remember, you won't like all the new things you try, but you will like some of them. And inserting a few new things regularly into your life will keep your perspective more positive and less headed toward depression.

Fill Your Toolbox

The next goal in the emotional/social area also fits in well with the above section:

Goal no. 3 – Gather lots of techniques.

I always see my job as equipping my clients to face whatever problems they may be dealing with. Since we all usually deal with multiple issues, I try to give them lots of different tools. Visualize yourself as having an antidepression toolbox. You want to fill it with as many tools as you can—because one implement won't work for every situation. You want to learn lots of techniques so if one doesn't work, you can put it back and try another.

Imagine you are a handyman (or woman!) and all you have in your toolbox is a hammer. That's great if you're hammering nails, but what if you need to tighten some screws, saw off some boards or patch some drywall?

Trying to use one tool for every job that arises is not only impractical; it's also not very smart. A good handyman is going to have a whole array of devices in his or her toolbox—screwdriver, wrench, laser level, measuring tape, etc.

In the same way, you need as many techniques to deal with depression as you can gather up. Some of them you'll use on a daily basis. Others will be used less frequently. Some methods won't work for you at all, and that's okay. Nothing works across the board for everyone. The point is to gather information and start trying some of these procedures. You'll cope much better if you've at least tested some of these tools, and don't wait till you're in the middle of a crisis to try a new one.

So have a central gathering place to store ideas and techniques. You can use a notebook, file folder, electronic device, etc. Just start a list and get in the habit of adding to it whenever you hear something promising. Remember, the technique doesn't have to be perfect, just a good possibility. That way when you've had a really bad day and can feel yourself heading toward a major negative mood, you can pull out your list of techniques and try some. Often just taking action is enough to make you feel better, but it's easier if you have a list of possible activities to choose from and don't have to come up with any on the spur of the moment.

So start filling your toolbox! You may find possibilities in this book, see things your friends do, hear about something on TV, read about something, etc. Start a list. I can pretty much guarantee if you don't write it down, you won't remember it when you really need it. I'm not prone to depression (which, as I've discussed, can affect your memory), but I'm not great at remembering things either. I've realized for years that if I don't make notes of things, they're usually gone pretty quickly. I have a smartphone, and I've developed the habit of jotting things down on the notepad if I'm out and about. That way I don't have to trust my memory, which is a good thing!

Don't Worry, Be Happy

Dealing with depression on a long-term basis can be, well, depressing. Your usual mood tends to be gloomy, sad, unhappy, dejected, and low. It's probably obvious to state this, but that is not a fun place to be. If you've been depressed for a long period of time, depression may have become your normal state. It doesn't have to be your *permanent* state however. I tell clients all the time, "You need to develop a new normal." This is possible, but it takes a lot of conscious effort. We are continually drawn to whatever our "normal" is unless we deliberately resist it. The good news is that if we oppose the old normal long enough and work on new habits, we can change and have a new, healthier normal.

So if you want to help yourself overcome depression, the next goal is

Goal no. 4 – Work on deliberately lifting your mood.

There are several ways to do this, and I'm going to make some suggestions for you to try (remember, more tools for your toolbox!).

1 – *Laugh regularly*. Watch funny, silly movies or comedies on TV.

The pioneer in this area was Norman Cousins, journalist and editor of the *Saturday Review*, who was given a few months to live in 1964. When told that he had little chance of surviving, Cousins developed a recovery program using doses of vitamin C, along with a positive attitude, love, faith, hope, and laughter induced by Marx Brothers films. "I made the joyous discovery that ten minutes of genuine belly laughter had an anesthetic effect and would give me at least two hours of pain-free sleep," he reported. "When the pain-killing effect of the laughter wore off, we would switch on the motion picture projector again, and not infrequently, it would lead to another pain-free interval" (*Anatomy of an Illness as Perceived by the Patient: Reflections on Healing*, by Norman Cousins).

There is truly power in laughter. Cancer Treatment Centers of America states

> Today more than ever before, people are turning to humor for therapy and healing. Medical journals have acknowledged that laughter therapy can help improve quality of life for patients with chronic illnesses. Many hospitals now offer laughter therapy programs as a complementary treatment to illness. Laughter therapy, also called humor therapy, is the use of humor to promote overall health and wellness. It aims to

use the natural physiological process of laughter to help relieve physical or emotional stresses or discomfort. Studies have revealed that episodes of laughter helped to reduce pain, decrease stress-related hormones, and boost the immune system in participants.

www.cancercenter.com

People who are depressed don't laugh that often, for obvious reasons. But laughter and humor can be hugely therapeutic. If they can be used to help cancer patients feel better, they can certainly help unhappy people improve their mood. If you're doubtful about this, watch the movie *Patch Adams* (another pioneer in the use of laughter for healing). So get into the habit of exposing yourself to things that are funny and make you laugh. Do this on a regular basis and you'll see an improvement in how you feel, emotionally and in other areas of your life as well.

2 – Be aware of what you take in—music you listen to, movies and TV programs you watch, and books and magazines you read. Be aware of how much "dark" TV, movies, or books you watch and read. Programs about violent crimes do not make you feel less depressed. Try some programs that have a feel-good component in them. A few that come to mind are *Undercover Boss, Biggest Loser, The Amazing Race*, and pretty much any comedy. I love Food Network, HGTV, and DIY network because they focus on changing things in a positive way. If you struggle with dark moods, programs like these are much better for you than the heavy crime shows.

You may also need to cut back on the hard rock if this is your music of choice. Try some new age music or Christian music instead. New age music is loosely defined as a style of chiefly instrumental music characterized by light melodic harmonies, improvisation, and natural sounds (such as running water, rain, wind, etc.). If you're not familiar with this, go to YouTube and search for "relaxation music" or "new age music." You also might try "Steven Halpern," who is one of my personal favorites for relaxation music.

As mentioned above, Christian music is a great way to lift your mood. If you haven't listened to any for a while, you may be in for a surprise. It's a lot more than hymns these days. Again, YouTube is a great way to explore this option a bit before you go out and spend any money. Type in "Praise and Worship Music" and see what comes up. Some artists and groups I like are Phillips, Craig and Dean, MercyMe, Sandi Patty, Steven Curtis Chapman, Kristian Stanfill, Point of Grace, Casting Crowns, and Amy Grant. There are lots of great artists and groups to choose from, so find some you like!

3 – *Pretend to be happy.* This goes back a few chapters ago to the always popular "fake it till you make it." I won't go into detail again here, but remember, make yourself smile! Ask yourself, "What would I be doing now if I were happy?" Then do that. It is truly amazing how effective this simple technique is. Act like a happy person long enough and you will eventually become, if not a completely happy person, at least a much happier one than you were in the beginning.

4 – *Spend time with friends and family* (if they are emotionally healthy). This is a technique that may need to be practiced with some caution. You can always change your friends, but you're stuck with family. So first, think about your friends. How do you feel when you're around them? Are they generally upbeat, positive people, or do they typically bring you down? If you usually feel worse after being around them, you may need to get new friends.

I'll share a personal example of this. Years ago I had a friend I used to work with. I'll call her Stephanie. I really liked Stephanie, she could be fun and good company, but she had one habit that drove me crazy. Her marriage was not great, and she was always telling me about it and asking my advice (this was before I was a therapist). I've never been big on giving unsolicited guidance, but when people ask me, I'll usually give an opinion. So I would think over her situation and give her some good (if I do say so myself!) suggestions. However, she would always come up with reasons why she couldn't follow them.

This was my first experience with a very common phenomenon in counseling—people pay to come in and see you, tell you their problems, ask for suggestions, and then don't follow them. It is extremely annoying (at least for me), and it happens on a surprisingly regular basis. Whenever I would make a suggestion for Stephanie, she would counter it with, "That sounds good, *but* I can't do it because..." or "Yes, *but* that won't work because..." You get the picture. In counseling, we call these people *yes butters*. Basically they want to complain about their problems and aren't really interested in doing anything to fix them.

They just want lots of sympathy and understanding—they pretty much enjoy their misery.

This frustrated the stuffing out of me! It got so bad that I really didn't enjoy being around Stephanie anymore and eventually eased out of the friendship. I didn't know as much about human nature back then as I do now, so I couldn't figure out what was going on. Why would she ask for my advice and then consistently not follow it? I understand it more now but still don't like it (and Ed was a huge *yes butter*!). Even though I didn't get all the dynamics of what was going on, I figured out that being with Stephanie made me feel stressed, frustrated, and annoyed. So I gave myself permission to greatly reduce the amount of time I spent with her. If you have a Stephanie in your life, you may need to do the same. Unfortunately, it's not as easy to get out of relationships with family members, but you may need to set some boundaries here as well.

Hopefully you have some relationships with friends and family that are supportive, encouraging, and generally positive. These are the people you want to be spending time with. And if you're like most of us, you may need to put that time on your calendar. If we wait for these lunches or dinners to happen by themselves, they often don't.

Think about someone you feel close to. It can be a family member or friend. When was the last time you spent a few hours with them? When I ask clients this question (including, "When was the last time you had a date night with your spouse?"), the answer ranges from weeks to years! We are all really busy these days. So don't wait for those times to just happen. Take the lead in setting something up. This will give you a chance to reconnect with a loved one, and I think you'll be glad you did.

5 – *Let the sun shine in.* It's often easy to know if someone is depressed by just walking into their home. I've seen it over and over. Sad people tend to draw the drapes and live in a space that is dark and gloomy. Because they don't feel up to doing anything, they huddle inside their caves and peer out timidly at the world. I've heard that this can feel cozy and inviting, but from what I've seen, this type of environment doesn't make anyone feel happier. So if this sounds like you, make an effort to let more light into your home—open up drapes and blinds, wash windows (maybe live dangerously and even open them!), and banish the darkness. If you really want to walk on the wild side, you can actually go outdoors! Take a walk, work in your yard, wash your car, etc. Just get outside and let the healing power of natural light go to work!

In case you think I'm overreacting here (because I really do like lots of natural light!), there is a form of depression called seasonal affective disorder (SAD). The depressive symptoms are generally the same as for a major depressive disorder, but the depressive episodes tend to appear at a particular time of year, usually fall and winter (when the days are shorter and there is less natural light available). The depression usually disappears in spring. This mood disorder is more pronounced in northern locations, and many people don't even know they have it till they move to Seattle or Michigan. One of the most common ways of dealing with SAD is to have the sufferer sit under a natural light lamp for forty-five minutes to an hour a day. This is called light therapy. So there is scientific evidence backing up the fact that we all need a certain amount of natural light and can become depressed when we don't get it.

6 – *Eat some chocolate.* Research shows that chocolate boosts serotonin in your brain, improving your mood. (This explains why I feel so good all the time!). Now don't get carried away here. You don't want to add a weight problem to your depression. Follow this advice in moderation. I have to be very firm with myself in this area, or I'd easily roll down my hallways! I'll give two personal examples of how I make this work.

I buy the little square Three Musketeers (the minis) and keep them in the freezer. I pull out one or two at a time and eat them—slowly! Since they're frozen, I have to nibble, or I risk breaking a tooth. I also keep a bag of Reese's Peanut Butter Mini Cups in my refrigerator (peanut butter doesn't freeze well). I'll also take out one or two and nibble on them gradually. Eating them this way allows me to really savor the chocolate without overdoing it on the sweets. (In case you're wondering, neither company is paying me to endorse their product—sadly).

7 – *Do something creative.* I read a study years ago that really interested me because it focused on women who practiced crafting. It found that women who did some type of crafting regularly (knitting, scrapbooking, cake decorating, etc.) had lower rates of depression than women who didn't. I've been trying to find that study ever since (see what happens when you don't write things

down?), so if any of you know where it can be found, please let me know.

This makes perfect sense to me because I love crafting and always feel better when I am able to do some. I believe, through personal experience and observation, that creating something gives you a feeling of accomplishment, pride, and empowerment. And all three of those emotions run counter to depression. So even if you don't see yourself as particularly artistic, try out some different crafts. There are lots to choose from. I'll list a few:

- Painting
- Gardening
- Sewing
- Knitting
- Quilting
- Crocheting
- Rubber stamping
- Cake decorating
- Woodworking
- Furniture making
- Stained glass
- Metal work
- Leather work
- Jewelry making
- Pottery

This is by no means an exhaustive list. The definition of crafting is "to use skill in making something," so I'm sure there are crafts I haven't thought of that could be included in the above list. The main point is that when you are done, there is a finished product that can be seen—something tangible you can look at and know that you created. And as I said earlier, it's very hard to feel proud and depressed at the same time, so crafting tends to cancel out depression.

8 – *Sing, sing a song.* I debated on whether or not to include this in the crafting section because in many ways it fits well there. I finally decided not to because crafting gives a concrete finished product and singing does not. However, like crafting, singing has huge antidepressant benefits. Research shows that singing produces endorphins, hormones that make you feel good. Singing can be done alone or with a group, like a choir. Either is good, but participating in a group has additional social benefits, like connecting with other people. Singing has also been shown to reduce muscle tension and invoke the relaxation response. Most people simply feel better after singing. Please note that you do not have to sing perfectly or even on key to experience these benefits. If you are self-conscious about people hearing, get into the habit of vocalizing in the shower or in your car. This is a habit worth developing. Singing has a calming, soothing effect, and it's very difficult to be relaxed and depressed at the same time.

9 – *Reach out and touch someone.* Our skin is the largest organ in our body, and we all use our sense of touch to comfort others and ourselves. Hugs, handshakes, pats, and caresses are all used to convey love and concern. Research shows that touch is hugely important in fighting depression. In fact, people who are touch deprived are more prone to physical diseases and emotional problems. Human and animal babies who are touch deprived don't even develop normally!

Touching others is something else depressed individuals generally don't feel like doing, but it can be vitally important to do it anyway. If you live with others, especially children, this is fairly easy to accomplish. Get into the habit of being more touchy-feely than you are normally. Hug your family members, put your arm around your spouse, trade off back rubs with your spouse and kids, and pat your children on the back or head as you walk by. This is an effort that gives benefits both ways, to you and to the person you're touching.

I thoroughly enjoyed the time when my sons were little. One of my favorite things to do was hold one (or both!) on my lap while I read them a story—anything by Dr. Seuss was a big hit. I loved the sense of physical connection I had with them. At times I miss that, but since they're twenty-one and twenty-three, sitting on my lap would be a bit problematic!

If you live alone, regular touch can be more difficult to find, so you may need to get a bit creative. Children are natural touchers, so volunteer at a local school or day care center for a few hours a week, or help out in the children's department of your church on a regular basis. If you have grandchildren, nieces, or nephews, or your neighbors or friends have young children, volunteer to babysit periodically. When you're with the children, read stories, put together puzzles, go to the park, play with blocks, etc. Once they get to know you, kids are great huggers!

10 – *Open up about your feelings*; however, don't become preoccupied with them. I discussed this in an earlier section, but it bears repeating. Depressed individuals have a bad tendency to keep things inside and brood obsessively

over them, otherwise called ruminating. Keeping things bottled up and going over and over them in a destructive manner is not helpful. I always encourage clients to find ways to express negative emotions as a tactic for dealing with them. I'm going to discuss a few options here.

First, have a regular pity party. This may sound odd, but it can be actually be helpful if done properly. So here are the rules. Really moan and groan and get it all out—and set a timer for fifteen minutes. When the timer goes off, the party is over for the day. You have to wait till tomorrow for the next one. This works because it's a way of letting off steam. It's acknowledging that things may be lousy and expressing how you feel about them. However, since there is a time limit, it doesn't get out of hand. I've had clients do this and be surprised by the fact that they really do feel better afterward.

Second, start journaling. This is a fairly easy thing for most people to do, and there are several ways you can do it. Use a notebook, computer, or password-protected flash drive. Please do not journal online unless you're comfortable with lots of people reading what you write. (There is no such thing as complete privacy online.) There are only two rules for journaling: always date your entries and don't worry about grammar, spelling, punctuation, or syntax. The reason for dating is so that you can look back later and, hopefully, see that you have made some progress. The rationale behind the second regulation is that this is supposed to be a spill-your-guts-and-emotional-dumping time. No one is going to be grading this, so just let things out. If you try journaling, be aware that it's most helpful if you do it on a regular basis. Once a month usually doesn't accomplish too much.

Third, talk it out. This is different from a pity party. Talking it out is expressing your frustrations and trying to verbally figure out what the specific issues are. Most people are usually good at expressing themselves in writing or speaking. A few do both equally well. So if writing isn't your thing, try this one. The beauty of talking it out is that you can do it even if you live alone. You can certainly talk to another person—if you have one who will listen and not judge. But if you don't have that, you can talk to your pet (animals are great listeners), your plants, or to an empty chair (imagine whoever you want sitting in it). The point here is to get it out of your system so it doesn't fester and brew inside you.

I'll give an example of how this can work. When my mom (Barb Green) was alive, she served as a volunteer at a woman's prison (Mabel Bassett) in Oklahoma City for years. She was interested in prisons and inmates and came across the following information one time. Studies show that there is a lower rate of violence in women's prisons than in men's, and there is one factor that seems to be important in causing the difference. Women complain more than men. Women moan, groan, and grumble to whoever will listen. Men tend to hold everything inside—until it all explodes outward. The thinking is the ongoing nitpicking women engage in acts as a safety valve and keeps things from detonating. So give it a shot! (Sorry, I don't have a copy of this study so can't verify that this information is accurate. I can, however, say that it makes sense.)

Hopefully some of the preceding tools will be ones you will try and use on a regular basis. Give them a shot and see how they work out. Remember, the goal is not to cope *perfectly* but to cope *better*, hopefully, after time, significantly better. Let's look at the next goal.

Get Up Close and Personal

One of the most common signs of depression is social withdrawal. People who are despondent can easily turn into hermits. I've never personally experienced it, but I've observed it in Ed and clients for years. Contact with the outside world is decreased over time until the person is virtually isolated. This is not helpful! I went to a positive psychology workshop one time and heard the phrase "There are no healthy hermits." I've tried to find out who said it (without success), but it's very true. We are designed to need regular contact with others. So here is your next goal:

Goal no. 5 – Connect with others.

This can be especially challenging to a depressed person, so here are some ways to attempt it:

1 – *Socialize with other people*. It's okay to start small. Take opportunities that are offered if it's too much to

initiate something on your own. Family (again, if they are emotionally healthy) is a good place to start, along with friends and coworkers. Most families have get-togethers from time to time—birthday parties, watching children playing sports, weddings, anniversary parties, eating out, etc. Resolve to participate in some of these. It may be scary, especially if you haven't been to an event in a while, so don't have unrealistic expectations. You're probably not going to have a fabulous time, and there may be awkward moments. Go anyway.

Keep in mind that the goal isn't to have the best time of your life. It's to get out of the house and reconnect with loved ones. If you're not sure on what to talk about and you don't want the focus to be on *you*, ask lots of questions about what's going on with *them*. Focus on listening attentively and chiming in occasionally. That's usually more than enough to keep the conversational ball rolling, and people will enjoy being around you.

If you have cut yourself from your friends, you may need to reestablish connections. Think about places your friends normally go (church, gym, restaurants, etc.) and try showing up there again. Or you could contact them and suggest getting together for a meal. Coworkers tend to go out to lunch or get together after work. When was the last time you joined them? They may have stopped asking you (especially if you've been turning them down for months), so you may need to take the initiative here. Try to ease yourself back into some social networks, but there is no need to overdo it. If you've been a recluse for a while, start slow. Try to get out once a week. After a few weeks, make an attempt to increase it to twice a week every other week or so. Don't worry, you don't have to turn into a social butterfly. Just come out of your cocoon on a more regular basis!

2 – A slightly different way to get the therapeutic effect of being close to loved ones is to *get a dog* and play with him/her several times a day. I've been making *canine prescriptions* for clients for years. Any pet can be therapeutic, but dogs are outstanding mood lifters. They always love you, are thrilled to see you, think you're wonderful, and give you a warm (sometimes overpowering!) welcome when you return. This can be especially helpful for some depressed individuals who have trouble getting along with others. Animals can be less threatening, and I have had many depressed clients tell me they get along much better with their pets than with their coworkers.

3 – *Remember it's not all about you.* One thing that can be very easy for depressed individuals to develop is tunnel vision. All they see is themselves and their issues. If your focus is all on you, it can be even easier to isolate yourself from others. Make an effort to direct your concentration to people around you on a regular basis. If you live with your family and have been depressed for a long time, odds are they feel neglected. Force yourself to talk and *listen* to them consistently. Your tendency will probably be to huddle in your chair or bed, but remember, this isn't helpful. It will be challenging at first, but make yourself spend regular time with each family member you live with. They probably miss you and will appreciate some attention from you.

It can be very easy to tell yourself that no one has problems like yours, and that may be true. But dwelling on them to the exclusion of all else only makes them seem bigger and more overwhelming. Sometimes the best thing you can do to make yourself feel better is to take the spotlight off yourself and turn it on someone else. The sad truth is that there is always someone in a worse position than you. So try to turn the focus off yourself periodically. It's good for you, and others around may appreciate it!

Prepare for the Long Haul

I've mentioned this earlier, and it bears repeating. Depression is a lonely battle and a solitary journey. Other people may be willing to help you, but beyond a certain point, you have to do things yourself. So here's the next objective:

> *Goal no. 6 – Develop a long-term attitude—this is a marathon, not a sprint.*

I really wish I could tell you that if you start doing the things I've suggested, you'll feel all better in a few weeks. Unfortunately, I can't. It is going to take time to heal. I frequently get asked how much time, which is understandable. My answer is always the same: I don't know. It's different for everyone, and a lot depends on how much effort you're willing to put into this. If you try some of these things once or twice and then stop, you're probably not going to notice much difference.

Your goal is to practice these new skills on a regular basis until you develop new, healthier habits. Prevailing research indicates it takes anywhere from twenty-one to sixty-six days to establish a different habit. The first few days need to be very consistent. After the first couple of weeks, you can miss a day here and there without much real damage.

You are going to have to be very patient and realistic with yourself. If you've suffered from depression for months to years, you're unlikely to feel better quickly—as much as you might want to. The attribute you're trying to acquire is *persistence*. My favorite definition for this is, "the quality of continuing steadily despite problems or difficulties." That's it in a nutshell. Picture yourself plodding on. Speed isn't important because this isn't a race.

Years ago I ran a marathon in Houston, Texas (don't remember which one—it was a long time ago!). I've run off and on for most of my life but had never done a marathon before and knew I needed to train well if I wanted to be standing at the end of it. I'll let you in on a somewhat embarrassing secret—I'm a *very slow* runner. It's a little more understandable now that I'm in my fifties, but this was true even in my twenties. From sad experience, I've learned to position myself at the back of the pack because if I don't, everyone passes me, and I do mean everyone. Little kids, heavy people, people in wheelchairs, and senior citizens—they all just zip by me. It used to be somewhat humiliating, but eventually I got used to it.

So I knew that I would be training for endurance and not speed. I did a good job getting ready and really enjoyed the race. People were cheering along the way, and it was fun! However, they closed the course after five hours, and I wasn't finished. I looked behind me and was somewhat surprised to see lots of people still running along with me. A big group of us finished the course after it was officially closed. We dodged cars and pedestrians and just kept chugging along. None of us got medals or trophies, but we did get the satisfaction of completing the race. The nice thing is that there was still a good group of people encouraging us on.

I've remembered that experience for years and often use it to help me keep going when I get discouraged. Frequently in life, it's not how well or fast or stylishly you finish that counts; it's just the fact that you didn't give up. That's the mentality you will need here because I can just about guarantee you'll get discouraged along the way. Just keep going! Enough baby steps add up to some pretty impressive progress, so keep marching along.

Be Realistic

One of the things you have probably figured out is, you can't change your past, and you may not be able to change your current circumstances—much. I have had clients tell me about truly horrendous events that happened to them in their past. I have felt genuine sympathy for them, but as much as I might want to, I can't change past occurrences. What we can affect is the present and the future. So here is your next goal:

> *Goal no. 7 – Accept what can't be changed and work with what you have.*

I've seen many clients, depressed or not, who really get into being victims. They spend a lot of time moaning and groaning about how unfair life is and what a rotten deal they have. Oftentimes they are right. Life can be pretty darn unfair. However, as I try to gently point out, some circumstances can't be changed, and endless complaining usually doesn't help. So if you're in a tough spot, alter what you can. Get a fresh perspective on your situation (talk to friends, family, or a professional) and adjust what is possible. Sometimes even small modifications can make a huge difference.

I'll give an example to explain what I mean. Years ago I had a client who hated his job. The people he worked with were very difficult, and it had gotten to the point where he dreaded going into work every day. However, his wife had a very serious disease, and his present company had excellent medical benefits. He knew that if he switched jobs, she would be viewed as having a preexisting condition that would not be covered by new insurance. So he was stuck in a job he hated.

We discussed several alternatives and then came up with a plan. The company he worked for was very large, and there were always positions available in other departments. He found one that sounded good, applied for it, and got it. In essence, he made a lateral move—same company, different position (and different coworkers), same salary, and same benefits. We were able to change his situation enough to make it much more workable for him, while staying within the parameters he needed.

Sometimes that's the best you can hope for. You can't completely change the situation as you might like, but you can tweak it enough to make it significantly better. Often depressed individuals don't think about this because they have such an all-or-nothing mentality. So look at whatever your current situation is and try to assess it objectively. What can't be changed, and what can? Very few circumstances are completely incapable of any modification. If you're having trouble thinking about this, impartially ask someone whose opinion you trust. By the way, this is a really good time to consult a professional. They'll be able to give a fairly neutral opinion. I'll address this more in the "Things That Can Help – Physical" section.

Let me give a word of caution here: if your spouse is the problem, I am *not* advocating an affair or divorce. In my opinion, an affair creates a lot more problems than it solves. I am not totally opposed to divorce (in some cases, that is the only option available), but it should never be entered into without a great deal of thought, prayer, and consideration.

We've looked at the emotional aspect pretty thoroughly. Now let's move on to the mental side.

It's A Mind Game

Remember that as I go through the rest of this book, I will explain new material, give a goal to strive for, and then discuss ways to help you reach that goal. So here is your first goal for the mental area:

> *Goal no. 1 – Work on identifying and changing your thinking.*

It's always been interesting to see how depression is perceived as an emotional problem. It certainly has an emotional aspect, but I strongly believe that, at the root, it's a *mental* issue. So people who are depressed are probably not going to change how they *feel* until they change how they *think*.

This can be a tough one to understand, especially if the depression is huge and has tentacles in every aspect of the person's life (the dark octopus). But here's how it works. We all have messages we give ourselves about, well, everything. These come from what is sometimes called *core beliefs*. These are beliefs we hold about life in general. You may not think you have them, but trust me, you do. Let me give some examples. I'll share some common positive and negative core beliefs.

Functional/positive:

- If you work hard, you can get ahead.
- My family will always love me, even if they don't agree with me.
- God will always love me and be there for me.
- If God closes a door, he opens a window.
- Things usually work out for the best.

Dysfunctional/negative:

- I'm so completely unlovable, it's no wonder I have no friends.
- If I'm not perfect in all ways, at all times, it's terrible!
- Everyone has to like me at all times, or something is wrong.
- I can never do anything right, so there's no point in trying.
- I'm terrible at (fill in the blank), and I'll never get any better at it.

Do any of these sound familiar? I've just listed a few, but we all probably have several dozen that guide our thoughts and feelings. Obviously, people who tend to be depressed have more dysfunctional/negative core beliefs. People who generally do not suffer from depression usually have more functional/positive ones.

Our core beliefs are hugely important. They determine the type of messages we give ourselves about life in general. Let me give some examples.

If I believe that life is generally fair and people are usually good, I'm probably going to be more motivated to try for that new job I've found. After all, I tell myself, I have lots of good experience, and my current boss and coworkers will give me good references. I'm smart, hardworking, and likable—they'd be crazy not to hire me!

Now let's look at the same example from a different perspective. If I believe that life is not fair and people are basically selfish and out to get me, I'm probably not likely to apply for a new job. After all, what's the point? I've heard that the people working there are real snobs, and I know that my boss and coworkers (who really hate me and have it in for me) would never give me a good recommendation. Besides, I really don't have that much experience. There will probably be lots of people applying who are more qualified that I am. So why bother?

Do you see the difference, and how core beliefs dictate the messages we give ourselves, the actions we take, and the way we feel about it all eventually? It's all related, and what we *think* leads directly to how we *feel*.

Things to help achieve goal number 1 (i.e., Work on identifying and changing your thinking.)

1. The first thing to do is identify the messages you are giving yourself. The easiest way to do this is to carry a notebook (or electronic device) around for a few days, and as you think of something you regularly tell yourself, write it down. At the end of a few days, you should have a good starting point.

2. Then come up with a different, positive, and functional message (which are now going to be called positive affirmations) to take the place of *each* negative, dysfunctional one. Remember, "Nature abhors a vacuum." What that means is that it's much harder to delete something than replace it.

3. Back up your new positive affirmation with some evidence.

I'll give some examples of how this should work.

> *Old negative/dysfunctional thought* – "I'm so stupid—I can never do anything right."
>
> *New Positive Affirmation* – "Actually, I'm pretty smart."
>
> *Evidence* – "I made a 3.5 GPA last semester, and my advisor said my grades will easily get me into graduate school"
>
> *or*
>
> "I got that big project at work finished early, and my boss commented on what a good job I had done."
>
> *Old negative/dysfunctional thought* – "I don't have any friends, and I probably never will. I'm such a loser, it's no wonder no one likes me."

New Positive Affirmation – "When I think about it, I realize I know several people who are friends and who like me."

Evidence – "Erica and Robin came over to my house last weekend. We went to the movies and came back to my place for a meal I had cooked. They both commented on what a good cook I am and said how much they enjoyed the day. I've been friends with them for several years."

Old negative/dysfunctional thought – "I completely screwed up that presentation at work. Everyone was laughing at me, and they all think I'm an idiot."

New Positive Affirmation – "Really I just messed up on one little part. About 95 percent of the presentation went very well."

Evidence – "My pages had gotten out of order, and I realized it quickly and fixed things. Yes, a few people laughed, but when I read from page 1 to page 5, it didn't make sense and was pretty funny. After I was finished, several of my coworkers told me what a good job I had done."

As you can see, this part is pretty simple to do; however, it can represent a profound mental shift and may seem scary and overwhelming at first. Don't get discouraged! Take a few days (even a week) to make your list of negative/dysfunctional thoughts. Try to get as many of them written down as you can. And don't worry if you don't get them all listed within the week. You can always add on to the list later—it's pretty much a work in progress. Then take a break for a day or two if you need it.

Okay, now it's time to tackle the harder part—coming up with a positive affirmation to replace each negative/dysfunctional thought and gathering evidence to back each one up. Please don't skip this step. It's very important. Be creative and think outside the box. You may need to get help at first, so don't be afraid to consult with family, friends, or coworkers. Take some time on this step because you need to do this well in order to be able reach goal number 2, which is coming up shortly.

Retrain Your Brain

This is actually part 2 of goal no. 1, the practical application part. Now that you have your list it's time to do some *cognitive restructuring*, which is a very complicated procedure. How do you do this you ask? Simple, take your list and read it out loud to yourself (just the positive affirmations) several times a day. There's one more thing that can help. Read it out loud while looking at yourself in a mirror. Yes, that's it—easy, uncomplicated, and very doable.

Here's the logic behind this step. Most of the time we acquire negative/dysfunctional messages pretty early in life, and they usually come from other people—like parents, siblings, teachers, schoolmates, etc. They are usually given verbally (so we hear them spoken), and often someone is looking at us (eye contact) when they speak them. So the best way to erase the old messages and replace them with new ones is to replicate (as closely as possible) the way they were originally given. Therefore, say the positive affirmations out loud while looking at yourself in a mirror. That way you have the spoken words and the eye contact. This may sound strange to you, but trust me, it works.

You may feel silly doing this. That's okay. Do it anyway. Remember, *any new behavior feels awkward and uncomfortable at first.* When you first tried to ride a bicycle, you probably didn't get it right the very first time. You may have fallen a few times, skinned your knee or elbow, and been really wobbly and erratic as you tried to master this new skill. What would have happened if you let that temporary discomfort stop you from trying to ride? You would never have learned to ride a two-wheeler, and you might have become convinced that you were stupid, incompetent, clumsy, etc. However, as you persisted, the wobbling grew less, and you stayed upright a lot more. Eventually, you didn't even need to think about it. Riding a bicycle became effortless. You may even have learned a few tricks like popping a wheelie (something I never mastered!). Practice may not make perfect (perfection is never the goal), but it does make things more easy, natural, and effortless.

So three times a day (minimum), take your list into the bathroom or bedroom and stand in front of a mirror. Then read it out loud while making eye contact with yourself (again, only the positive affirmations). Also, if an old negative/dysfunctional thought pops into your head during the day, immediately counter it with the positive affirmation on your list. What this means is that at first you'll need to carry your list around with you (and by the way, you can put the list on index cards or an electronic device). But after a while, you won't even need to consult the list—you'll know it, and the new Positive Affirmation will pop into your head without much effort.

Commit to doing this for the next few months. If you have been depressed for a long time, a year would be better. This exercise only takes a few minutes a day, but the results are completely worth it. You're reprogramming your brain, and while this isn't a complicated procedure, it does need to be done consistently over a period of time.

I know that sometimes it's hard to think of what to say on your own. So take a look at the appendix. I have a list of positive affirmations for depression there that should help.

Accentuate the Positive

I often caution my clients to remember that we *choose* what we will believe and what we pay attention to. Thoughts lead to feelings that lead to actions.

I usually get some arguments from my chronically depressed clients over this one, but I firmly believe it's true. We choose our beliefs a lot more than most of us are aware of, and I can give a great example.

Last year I went to the ICBCH (International Certification Board for Clinical Hypnotherapy) annual meeting in Dallas. There were several extra events we could go to, and one I attended was a firewalking event at the Firewalking Institute of Research and Education. There was a dinner first, and then those who were interested were shown how to walk across a bed of live, hot, glowing coals.

Logically and rationally, this does not seem like a good thing to do. The coals were real, and we were walking barefoot. A large part of the experience was being able to convince yourself that you could do it. So basically we were all *choosing* to believe we could walk across the coals and not be hurt, and we all did!

This is a more extreme example than most of us are used to (by the way, I highly recommend the experience if you're ever in the area—their Web site is www.firewalking. com), but the principle is the same for other events as well. Any of you who have ever parented a teenager have probably had an experience similar to the following.

You tell your fifteen-year-old that relatives are in town and everyone is meeting the next day at Grandpa and Grandma's for dinner. Your teen was planning on doing something with his friends and argues vigorously with you, but you stand firm. Your son (we'll call him Paul) moans, groans, sulks, and complains the rest of the day and the next one. He keeps saying how boring family events are and how much he hates going to them. You all go anyway, and Paul sits off by himself, texts his friends (whenever he thinks you're not looking), and refuses to interact with anyone. Even though the rest of you are having fun, and there are relatives his own age there, Paul proceeds to have a miserable time and complains about it all the way home.

The rest of the family thoroughly enjoyed themselves. Why was Paul's experience so different? Because he convinced himself it wouldn't be any fun, and he then made that belief come true (this is the self-fulfilling prophecy I talked about earlier). Paul's beliefs dictated his actions, which then dictated his experiences/feelings.

This happens all the time! We all do this consistently, and that's why our beliefs are so important. They have a huge impact on our emotions. We choose what we will believe, which then affects how we feel. So in essence, we choose what we will feel for the most part as well.

I frequently tell clients that if they are pessimists, they would be better off retraining their thinking and becoming more optimistic. If all we see in any given situation are the bad things (and believe me, they're there!), it's very easy to convince ourselves that it's *all* bad. We can get to the point where we simply don't see any of the positive aspects of a situation. And if all we focus on are things that are negative, bad, and horrible, pretty soon life itself becomes negative, bad, and horrible.

My point here is that we largely choose what we think, believe, focus on, are aware of, and feel. If that's the case, why not choose to zoom on some positive points and try ignoring (or at least downplaying) all the negative ones?

Martin Seligman talks about this in his excellent book *Learned Optimism* (New York: Vintage Books, 2006, 4–5). He talks about the fact that he has studied optimists and pessimists for twenty-five years. He states,

> The defining characteristic of pessimists is that they tend to believe bad events will last a long time, will undermine everything they do, and are their own fault. The optimists, who are confronted with the same hard knocks of this world, think about misfortune in the opposite way. They tend to believe defeat is just a temporary setback, that its causes are confined to this one case. The optimists believe defeat is not their fault:

circumstances, bad luck, or other people brought it about. Such people are unfazed by defeat. Confronted by a bad situation, they perceive it as a challenge and try harder.

Later on in the book, he makes the statement, "Pessimists can in fact learn to be optimists, and not through mindless devices like whistling a happy tune or mouthing platitudes but by learning a new set of cognitive skills" (p 5).

I agree wholeheartedly with his assessment, which leads to

Goal no. 2 – Learn to be more of an optimist than a pessimist.

If this is totally new to you, start small. Make a point to look for the good in situations and people. This will probably take practice and may be difficult at first. And to be frank, some situations and people don't have much good that leaps to the eye. You may have to really dig.

I'll give an example that may help. When I was working on my bachelor's degree in early childhood education, one teacher was talking about positive reinforcement for kids in the classroom. She made the statement that some kids, even in kindergarten, didn't bring a lot of good qualities to the table. But she said that when they did something even halfway good, it was vital to recognize and encourage it so they would do more of the same. What we wanted to do was encourage new habits (good ones) in the children.

It's the same idea for becoming an optimist. Whenever you see something good recognize it, acknowledge it, make a note of it, etc. It can be something simple—your coworker turned down her music the first time you asked her, the waiter apologized for his mistake and corrected your order quickly, your boss complimented you on the presentation you gave, etc.

Sometimes, because this is a completely foreign mindset, you may need a little help. That's okay. Learn to ask for it. Find friends, coworkers, or family members who seem pretty upbeat and explain what you're trying to do. Be honest. "I don't always see the positive things in a situation, but I'm trying. Would you help me by pointing out some things I may be missing?" After a while, it will come more naturally. I promise.

At this point, I'm sure you're asking what you should do when the negative things leap out at you, and they will. It's simple. When a negative thought pops into your head, find something positive to counteract it with. I'll give some examples.

"I can't believe my son went off the school and left his room in such a mess." (negative thought) Now for a positive thought to counteract and/or balance the negative one. "Well, he's usually not this messy. I know he was hurrying to get to school early because his coach had asked him to help organize the baseball equipment. He's really a good kid although he can be a bit absentminded at times. I'll text him a reminder about his room."

"What an awful day! It's wet, dark, and dreary outside—great! There go my plans to work in the yard and exercise." (negative thought) Now for a positive one.

"However, we do need the rain. The yard was looking dry. And while I may not be able to do yard work, I can organize the garage. I'll open the door and enjoy the rain while I work—and watch my lawn get watered! The weather report says the rain should clear up later this afternoon. I'll ride my bike then."

Hopefully you get the idea. The object is not to completely ignore or be unaware of the bad things around you. Instead you want to become *more* aware of the good things. You're working to change your focus and to turn the spotlight on the positive. Remember, thoughts lead to feelings that lead to actions.

If your thoughts are filled with negative ideas and perspectives, you will feel negative, depressed, and down, which will lead you to *not* doing things that can help you feel better. So work on seeing the glass half full rather than half empty. It will be well worth it!

Rumination Is Ruinous

A trait that I frequently see in depressed individuals is a tendency to ruminate—to brood over and over about the negative situation, belief, or event. Replaying it endlessly in their mind, mulling it over angrily, dwelling on the unfairness of the situation repeatedly. Please pay attention to what I am about to say. *Ruminating over negative situations does not help*. In fact, research shows that it makes things worse.

When something bad happens to us, it's normal to be obsessed with it for a while. We tell our friends and family and repeat it to ourselves several times, maybe posting it on Facebook as well. There's nothing wrong with this. For most of us, it's a way of processing and coming to terms with what happened. It also helps to get sympathy and understanding from others. *But* if weeks after the bad thing happened we're still dwelling on it and are unable to let it go, something needs to change.

So here is goal no. 3 – *Don't allow yourself to ruminate in a negative manner.*

Again, I'm going to summarize some of Martin Seligman's book *Learned Optimism.* He states, "Ruminators who are pessimists are in trouble. Their belief structure is pessimistic, and they repeatedly tell themselves how bad things are" (New York: Vintage Books, 2006, 82). He explains how pessimism and rumination lead to depression.

> First, there is some threat against which you believe you are helpless. Second, you look for the threat's cause, and if you are a pessimist, the cause you arrive at is permanent, pervasive, and personal. Consequently, you expect to be helpless in the future and in many situations, a conscious expectation that is the last link in the chain, the one triggering depression. The expectation of helplessness may arise only rarely, or it may arise all the time. The more you are inclined to ruminate, the more it arises. The more it arises, the more depressed you will be. Brooding, thinking about how bad things are, starts the sequence. Ruminators get this chain going all the time.
>
> (New York: Vintage Books, 2006, 83)

I have seen this sequence in depressed individuals countless times, and I believe there are two causes of negative rumination. One is simply *learned habits.* People who are pessimists develop defeatist thinking patterns pretty early in life. These habits can be very strong and pervasive, but the good news is that, like any habit, they can be changed or broken.

The other cause I have seen and experienced is *spiritual warfare*. Satan is described as the prince of this world (John 14:30). He has the power to attack our thoughts and to try and throw us off balance. The Bible makes this threat plain elsewhere:

> Finally, be strong in the Lord and in his mighty power. Put on the full armor of God so that you can take your stand against the devil's schemes. For our struggle is not against flesh and blood, but against the rulers, against the authorities, against the powers of this dark world and against the spiritual forces of evil in the heavenly realms.
>
> Ephesians 6:10–12 (NIV)

1. I have experienced times in my life when I have felt as if I was being bombarded relentlessly by destructive, negative thoughts. I have heard clients, family, and friends say the same. Personally, I seem more prone to this when I am angry (even justifiably) and am holding on to that anger along with unforgivingness and bitterness. Satan's attacks on our minds can be harsh and ruthless. Often I have not been able to break through this thought pattern to stop it by myself. So I have found myself praying something along these lines, "Lord, please redirect my thoughts. I'm tired of thinking about _____. It's not helping the situation, but those thoughts keep popping into my mind. I need your help."

   I believe God honors those prayers—I know he has for me. *But* it's not always quick or easy.

Sometimes I have literally run through the above prayer twenty or thirty times *in an hour*. Keep asking for help. God will keep providing it.

2. Something else you can do to break that chain of thoughts. *Take an action that puts a physical stop to it*. I'll give some examples to show you what I mean.

- Stand up (if you're sitting) and yell, "Enough!" Walk into another room and start doing something else.

- Wear a rubber band on your wrist, and when the negative thoughts starting flooding your mind, pop the rubber band (hard!) and repeat a catch-word or catchphrase such as
    - I'm done with that!
    - Stop!
    - No more!

- If you're home, go outside for a walk, run, or bike ride—weather permitting. Taking your dog for a walk is always good too.

- If you live in the country, go outside and pull some weeds or chop some wood.

- I've advised lots of clients to get a punching bag (like they have in gyms) and hang it in their extra bedroom or garage. Get a pair of boxing gloves, and when angry/negative thoughts start overwhelming you, put on the gloves and go whack away at the bag. The physical release feels great!

3. Another thing that can be helpful is to find some *positive activity* you can do to counter the negative thoughts. If you think about it you can usually

find someone whose situation is worse than yours. Try to come up with something to do that will help them. This works wonders in getting your mind off yourself. I'll give some examples below.

- Find an organization such as Habitat for Humanity (if you're handy with tools) or your local animal shelter (if you're an animal lover) and volunteer on a regular basis.

- You've heard that your neighbor is in the hospital for a week or is serving in the military and is gone for several months. Contact his wife and volunteer to mow the lawn while he's away. Then show up and do it!

- Contact your friend who is a single parent and offer to run errands for him/her when you're out running your own. They will truly appreciate it!

The point is that when we take our focus off ourselves and look at others, we realize that our situation is not the worst in the world. It truly helps keep things in perspective and keeps our viewpoint more realistic. Sometimes talking about anything else is helpful. We can get sick of thinking about our own situation. So call a friend or family member and talk with them, preferably about another topic. Ask them about their life. Usually hearing about someone else's problems makes our own seem less insurmountable.

4. Often when our thinking goes automatically to the negative side, we tend to not see the good things in our life, and they are there! So something that

can help is to *keep a gratitude log*. This is pretty simple, and I have a place for it in the workbook. Every day jot down three things you are grateful for. I'll give some examples.

- Good health
- My education
- The house I live in
- My job
- My family
- My friends
- The country I live in
- My children
- The access I have to entertainment experiences
- The educational opportunities I have
- The church I attend and the spiritual guidance I receive there
- My sense of humor and fun

You get the idea? Many of these are things we take for granted and aren't really aware of, but we would certainly miss them if they were taken away. So make it a point to develop an attitude of gratitude, and learn to be aware of your many blessings. This is one of the best things you can do. Stop ruminating over the negative things in your life.

Choose to Chill

S omething health-care providers are learning is that stress affects depression and depression affects stress. Let me give you some facts from a report by the American Psychological Association entitled "Stress in America."

Depression is often exacerbated by stress. Those who suffer from this condition report that they are unable to take the necessary steps to relieve their stress or improve their health and, therefore, engage in maladaptive coping behaviors.

People suffering from depression report significantly higher average stress levels than the rest of the population. People with depression are more likely to report the following:

- Feeling overwhelmed
- Feeling dissatisfied with their lives
- Feeling dissatisfied with family relationships

- Feeling lonely or isolated as a result of stress
- Having tried to reduce their stress levels with less success
- Stress level having a very strong impact on their physical health

The APA further states that certain categories of people, such as those suffering from a chronic illness (I'm putting depression in this category), are at heightened risk of experiencing serious consequences of stress that is too high and appears to be taking a toll on their emotional and physical health ("Stress in America: Our Health at Risk," January 11, 2012).

You've probably figured it out by now, but here is your next goal:

Goal no. 4 – Learn to manage your stress.

Let's face it. We live in a society filled with stress! There's pretty much no way to avoid it, so the best thing to do is learn ways to manage it (so it won't manage us!).

I've taught stress management courses for several years, so let's start with the basics. What is stress? The best definition I've found is, *more demands made on us than we have resources to cope with*. Think about it. What do your days usually look like? Nonstop work, chores, activities, and demands on your time; or easy schedules, lots of free time, and a nice, nondemanding job?

Most of us fall into the first category. We tend to have more demands than we have time or resources to fill them. So how do we respond to those unending demands? Symptoms of stress are pretty universal. See if any of the following sound familiar:

- Headache
- Chest pain
- Fatigue
- Change in sex drive
- Stomach upset
- Sleep problems
- Anxiety
- Restlessness
- Difficulty concentrating and/or lack of motivation
- Irritability or anger
- Sadness or depression
- Change in eating habits
- Angry outbursts
- Drug or alcohol abuse
- Tobacco use
- Social withdrawal

The above are some of the symptoms, but how do you know if you really are stressed, and just how much stress you have? Glad you asked.

In 1967, psychiatrists Thomas Holmes and Richard Rahe decided to study whether or not stress contributes to illness. They surveyed more than five thousand medical patients and asked them to say whether they had experience any of a series of forty-three life events in the previous two years.

Each event, called a life change unit (LCU), had a different weight for stress. The more events the patient added up, the higher the score. The higher the score and the larger the weight of each event, the more likely the patient was to become ill.

I like the the Holmes and Rahe Stress Scale because it's very concrete and easy to understand. When I taught stress management, I gave it to my students every semester. It's a good thing to take on a regular basis to see where you fall and how you're coping with life in general. You can find it easily online, and it's free to take.

Okay, you've figured out you have a lot of stress in your life. Now what? Below I'm going to list some of my favorite stress busters. I believe it's important to have more than one because nothing works in every situation. Hopefully you'll find some of them helpful.

1. *Practice deep breathing.* With my clients, I start things on a very basic level—breathing. Deep breathing is one of the best ways to lower stress in your body. This is because when you breathe deeply, it sends a calming, soothing message to your brain. Your brain then sends this message to your body. I've seen amazing results from people who learn to take a break when they feel stress coming on and do some deep breathing exercises.

    Try this when you get stressed. Close your eyes and take a few deep breaths in and out. Repeat this mantra (or something similar) as you breathe. "I breathe stress out, I breathe relaxation in." To take it a step further, visualize the stress coming out of your body as a red mist. Visualize the relaxation coming in as a cool green mist. Taking a couple of minutes during the day to do this can make a world of difference.

This is especially good because when we get tense, we often start taking short, shallow breaths, which doesn't help the situation. Breathing exercises are a good way to relax, reduce tension, and relieve stress. Deep breathing is also easy to learn. Most of us already have it figured out! You can do it whenever you need, and no special tools are required.

2. *Exercise regularly.* Yes, there's that dreaded word, but I guarantee that it works! The key to getting a regular exercise program going is to find something that works for you. I don't care if something works for your mother or best friend. If you don't enjoy it, you're not going to do it.

So here's the Dr. Rich wisdom on exercise.

A – In my experience, people fall into one of three groups when it comes to exercise.

- *Large-group people* – They usually prefer some type of class.
- *Small-group people* – They like to work out with a few friends.
- *Solo exercisers* – They typically like to go it alone.

I believe it's critical to figure out what type you are, because if you're in the wrong setting, you won't enjoy it and will likely end up quitting. (By the way, I'm a solo exerciser. I absolutely hate classes, and the few times I've tried them, I've ended up dropping out). Figure out what works for you and stick to it.

B – Do you prefer to work out at home or at a facility (like a gym)? If you like to exercise at home, do you prefer indoor or outdoor? Either is fine. It's just helpful to know your preference. Just be aware that both groups need a plan B. If you like to go to the gym, what are you going to do when you can't go due to bad weather, a sick child, or a nonfunctioning car? And if you're strictly an outdoor person, what is your backup plan when the weather is too wet or icy to do your regular routine?

I'm an at-home person, and I have indoor and outdoor exercise that I do. I typically run or walk in the mornings and then try to jump on my rebounder (a small mini-trampoline) later in the day or use one of my exercise DVDs. I strongly encourage people to have several options because, if you're like me and really don't enjoy exercising, the slightest excuse can be used to not do it. "Oh, darn, I have to wait for the repair man—looks like I won't be able to make it to the gym today." However, if you have at-home options handy, you can simply make another choice.

C – As I mentioned above, I'm not a person who loves to exercise. I see people who happily proclaim that they love to work out and get hot and sweaty—what's wrong with them! That is *completely* not me. However, years ago, I discovered a simple truth—I feel and function better in all areas when I exercise regularly. It's still not my favorite thing, but I do it—daily. I realized that I was making things harder for myself by constantly saying "I *hate* exercising!" It was completely true, but it wasn't helping. So I decided to reprogram my mind when it comes to working out. I now have two exercise sayings I tell myself on a regular basis:

- I love the results that exercise produces, and,
- I don't have to like it. I just have to do it.

I wanted to quit being negative in my approach to working out but realized that I would never be able to truthfully say that I loved it. However, I do love what happens when I keep fit—hence, saying no. 1. The second saying I use for exercising and other things in my life that I just have to get through. I've shared them with clients over the years, and people seem to find them helpful—I know I have!

This section is also addressed in the "Things That Can Help – Physical" section.

3. *Get enough sleep.* This can be difficult when you're extremely stressed about a situation, but staying awake all night isn't helpful either. Stress and insomnia have a definite connection, and it's a circular one. If you're really stressed, you tend to lie wide-eyed and stare at the ceiling. When you get up the next morning, you're tired and worn out. This *decreases* your coping abilities and increases your stress level. That night you're more stressed and have trouble sleeping...you get the picture.

WebMd lists the following mental symptoms sleeplessness (Peri, Camille, 2010. "What Lack of Sleep Does to Your Mind." WebMd):

- It slows down your thought processes.
- It impairs memory.
- It makes learning difficult.

I'm not going to talk about ways to sleep better here because this topic is addressed extensively in the "Things That Can Help – Physical" section. However, I am going to use this book as a platform for one of my pet peeves—children not being allowed to nap. When kids don't get enough sleep, it causes stress in the entire family!

I have believed this to be a serious issue for years, and recent research appears to be backing me up. I was fortunate enough to be a stay-at-home mom when my sons were growing up, and naptime was an important part of their day. I structured my day around being home after lunch so David and Josh could get their daily siestas.

Just a note on individual differences here. I don't believe I ever had to tell David to take a nap. When he was younger, he would simply head to his bed after lunch and would routinely sleep for several hours every afternoon. As a college student, he still does this whenever possible. He will remove his contacts, put on PJs, close his blinds, and happily climb into bed. I've mentioned to him a few times that most people simply stretch out on the couch to catch a few zzz's during the day. His response is, "Mom, I want to get the full experience."

Josh was always another matter altogether. He was never interested in napping, but I could tell that he needed it. The problem was getting him to be still long enough to doze off. I finally hit on a foolproof way to get him to relax. I would lay down with him on a bed and throw my leg over his lower body, and put my arm over his chest. I found that if I held him quiet for a few minutes, he would eventually fall asleep. He never slept as long as David, but he was always in a much better mood after snoozing for an hour or so.

Children need regular naps! Whenever I am in a mall or store in the early afternoon and see a mom or dad dragging a crying child around, it's all I can do not to tell the parent to take that youngster home and put him or her in bed! *Science Daily* states that toddlers between two and a half and three years old who miss only a single daily nap show more anxiety, less joy and interest, and a poorer understanding of how to solve problems. The article further says, "Insufficient sleep in the form of missing a nap taxes the way toddlers express different feelings, and, over time, may shape their developing emotional brains and put them at risk for lifelong, mood-related problems" (University of Colorado at Boulder. "Nap-deprived tots may be missing out on more than sleep." *ScienceDaily*, 21 Jan. 2012. Web. 20 Aug. 2013.)

Parents.com (Kahlenberg, Rebecca R. "Nap Time." 2013) addresses this further. "Research suggests that physical and mental development takes place when kids sleep—both at night and during the day," says Daniel Lewin, PhD, director of pediatric behavioral sleep medicine at Children's National Medical Center in Washington DC. What's more, studies find that kids who nap have longer attention spans and are less fussy than those who don't. And perhaps the best reason of all, "When kids rest during the day, they tend to sleep longer and more peacefully at night."

My point in all this is to show, again, the connection between stress and lack of sleep—and lack of sleep and stress. It happens in adults, but it is also very present in children. Getting enough sleep is extremely important no matter what your age. And by the way, referring back to the previous section, getting regular exercise will also help you sleep better!

4. *Eat right.* If your stress level is high, it can be helpful to look at your diet. Often stress can cause us to overeat in an attempt (a bad one!) to cope. I've known many people who run to the refrigerator or ice cream stand when their lives turn hectic. Trust me on this (as one who has been there). Overeating to cope with stress is a very short-term solution at best. Yes, chowing down on sweets and carbs makes you feel good at the moment, but this is the type of action that will always come back to bite you. Really make an effort to avoid it.

If certain foods are a problem for you, don't bring them into your house. If you have a particular food craving, try this trick. Resist it for fifteen minutes. Use that time to start doing something else productive (cleaning out a drawer, checking your e-mail, etc.). If it's true hunger, the feeling will still be there when the fifteen minutes is up. If it's just a craving due to boredom, stress, or something else that is non-hunger related, it will usually be gone before the fifteen minutes elapse. This topic will be addressed more in depth in the "Things That Can Help – Physical" section.

5. *Connect with friends and family.* Stress can make it difficult for us to think clearly and objectively. We can get so caught up in a hectic situation that we often make it worse than it needs to be. This is when it's very helpful to spend some time with loved ones—for several reasons. It's good to know people care about you, they can give you an objective perspective on your situation, sometimes just having a sounding board can help you sort things out, and being with people you care about (and who care about you) can give you an emotional break from your situation. So when things get to be too much, try to get together with some loved ones—eat dinner, go to a movie, have a drink together, go for a drive, have a picnic, etc. I do this frequently, and it always helps me!

6. *Take time for hobbies and pastimes.* Remember the saying "All work and no play makes Jack a dull boy (or Jill a dull girl)"? There's a lot of truth to that. If all we do is go to work and take care of household things, we get into a routine—and one that can quickly become stale and boring. There's

a great booklet by Charles E. Hummel called *The Tyranny of the Urgent.* In it he talks about how we all let things that really shouldn't be that important get to the top of our priority list (IVP Books, April 19, 1994). I'm not saying we should quit our jobs or neglect household maintenance, but there needs to be a balance in our lives. What things do you do just because you enjoy them (and watching TV doesn't count!)? If you're like many of my clients, you've become so busy that you don't have any hobbies—or you haven't for years. If this is the case for you, it's time to reevaluate. Read on!

7. *Put fun in your schedule.* This one really goes with number 6, but for clarity, I've separated them. Have you ever watched a group of young children for a while? It doesn't matter what nationality or social economic status they come from, they will all eventually start doing one thing—playing. Children instinctively are drawn to playing and having fun. And I think because we associate play and fun with children, we seem to think we need to outgrow it when we become grownups. How depressing! Play and fun are essential parts of being a balanced person. When we don't have these two elements in our lives, we get out of whack (that's the technical term for it). So don't be afraid to put fun back in your life. It's not just for kids!

Often adults seem almost afraid to play and have fun and aren't sure where to even begin. So I've listed some things that are playful and fun for lots of people to give you a starting point. These won't all work for you, but try a few and see how they go. Add your own things to the list as you think of them as well.

- Garage selling – Having one or going to some
- Dance lessons
- Cooking lessons
- Flying a kite
- Parasailing
- Crafting
- Playing golf, tennis, racquetball, basketball, softball, baseball, or volleyball
- Cake decorating
- Hunting
- Archery
- Boxing
- White-water rafting
- Scrapbooking
- Antique shopping
- Photography
- Going to a concert, play, or opera
- Having a picnic
- Going to the beach
- Traveling

I could go on for pages, but you get the idea. Life is not all about work—or shouldn't be. If your life is stressful, check to see if you've made time for fun and play. If you haven't, it's not too late to put them in your schedule.

8. *Help others on a regular basis.* This one is pretty self-explanatory, so I'm not going to go to great

length. There's nothing that quite puts our own situations in perspective as looking at someone else's problems. I have regularly felt fairly sheepish at how overwhelmed I was by my own circumstances—and then went to church or turned on the news and heard about someone else's. It makes me realize the wisdom of the saying, "Things could always be worse." So make a point of helping out others. It's the right thing to do, and it helps you look at your position with a fresh eye.

9. *Get clutter under control.* This topic is covered at more length in the "Things That Can Help – Physical" section. However, it also applies here (some areas overlap), so I'll address it briefly. As stated elsewhere, I firmly believe that clutter oppresses the spirit. So much so that I regularly make an attempt to keep it under control—in my home, garage, and office. It's a constant battle because clutter is devious and has a habit of sneaking up on you.

My late husband Ed was a keeper. Nothing was ever thrown out. I found out later that this is a characteristic of obsessive compulsive personality disorder, something I believe Ed suffered from. After his death, I went through the house, garage, attic, and shed and threw or gave away over sixty boxes of *stuff!* I can't tell you how liberating it felt. Today my house is pretty clutter free, and I work to keep it that way. It's not pristine or museum like—people do live in it after all—and a small amount of disorder is unavoidable. But now my home is warm, inviting, and a haven.

If the clutter monster has taken over your life, I urge you to fight back. It can be overwhelming at first, so I suggest starting small. I often advise clients to start with straightening out one drawer. That's small and doable, and when you're done, you can see real change. In fact, you'll probably stop to open it and look in whenever you walk by, just because it feels so good! Then do another few drawers, next a closet or bookshelf, then a room, and so on. Your house won't be tidy and organized overnight, but given enough time, it will happen. Once it's neat and uncluttered, make a regular effort to keep it that way. I often suggest that clients have ten to fifteen minutes of family cleanup time. Set a timer for ten to fifteen minutes and during that time the whole family goes through the house picking things up, putting them away, folding and storing, throwing away, etc. If everyone participates, ten minutes can make a big difference. And if this happens several times a week, the house stays pretty tidy and manageable.

10. *As much as possible, avoid negative situations and people.* This can be tricky if the negative people in your life are family. Obviously you can't avoid them forever, but you can limit contact with them. And if you're married to a negative person, it's very important that you balance that out with other positive relationships. Let me be

very clear here. I'm *not* suggesting you start an affair because your spouse is not a fun person to be around. I'm talking about friendships that will help you keep your perspective when you feel overwhelmed by constant destructive input from your significant other.

And what if your job is a negative situation? This can also be problematic. Quitting your job because your boss is a jerk or your coworkers are downers may not be the best response. In these economic times, it's usually best to have another job lined up before giving up the one you already have. Try talking to the person or people who are making things difficult for you. Appeal to your supervisor or head of your department—if you're a valuable employee, they won't want to lose you and may be willing to make changes to keep you on board. If you work for a large organization, you may be able to find another position within the same company. Check with Human Resources to see if something else is available. It's always a good idea to keep your resume and contacts up to date. That way if your job becomes unbearable, you can start looking for a new one.

11. *Seek out the positive.* This one goes along with the number 10. If you feel that you're surrounded by negative people and/or situations, you may need to actively look for upbeat ones. Do you know anyone who smiles a lot? Which people make you feel good after spending time with them? What situations are enjoyable and fun for you? Take

a look at your life—whom do you spend your time with, and what activities pop up frequently on your schedule? Are they helpful, affirmative, and encouraging? If not, it may be time to make some changes. Life is too short to spend it sad and miserable!

12. *Learn to use some visualization techniques*, such as the following:

(I use these with clients often in hypnosis for stress management).

- If things seem overwhelming, visualize yourself in a box and picture yourself drilling holes in the box.

- Picture whatever is causing you distress and put it in a small chest. Flip the latches closed and lock the lid with a key. Tie large hot-air balloons to the handles and, after a moment, let go of the chest. Watch it float slowly away until it drifts completely out of sight.

- Picture a safe place for you. It can be anywhere, real or imaginary. A quiet forest, a deserted beach, your grandmother's kitchen, your own private castle, or a fluffy, white cloud. Imagine it in as much detail as possible. Get sights, sounds, textures, and smells to make it as vivid as can be. Whenever things become too much and you need an escape, close your eyes and see yourself in your safe place for a few minutes.

- Have you even been to a water park that has a lazy river? You get on an inner tube or flotation device and gently drift around the river. It's not going too fast, but it is moving. You feel relaxed and peaceful. Visualize yourself in that situation—floating slowly and easily along the waterway. You can also imagine the water sweeping all your stressors away.

- If you have a tough time with visualization, try this. Get online and go to YouTube. Search for something along the lines of "relaxation videos for stress" or "guided relaxation for stress management." You'll want to do these alone (unless people around you want to join in), but just follow the instructions on the videos. I'm not going to put any specific titles here because they change so quickly, but you should be able to find several that will help. There are all different lengths as well, so you can find one that works for the time you have. Once you find a few you like, make a note of them or bookmark them if you know how to do that.

Visualization is a great way to manage stress, but like any new skill, it can be challenging at first. If you decide to try it, commit to practicing it several times a week for two to three weeks. By the end of that time, you should have a handle on the technique and should see a real difference in your stress level!

Develop an Attitude of Gratitude

One of the things I see often in clients who are depressed is a real discontent with their situation. This happens to most people from time to time and, on an infrequent basis, is pretty normal for everyone. However, some people make a practice of this and are *never* happy no matter what their circumstances. If you fall into this category, you need to be careful—this personality trait is a recipe for unhappiness and depression, and you would be wise to work on changing it.

Try this useful exercise to see where you are. On a scale of 1 to 100, how happy are you—right now? (100 being perfectly, utterly happy, and 1 being totally and completely miserable).

Now you have your score. Great! Here's part 2. List everything it would take to make you significantly happier—yes, everything! Take some time to think about it and, above all, be as honest as you can be.

Okay, look over your list. What do you have listed, and how realistic are the items? Are entries likely to happen eventually given enough time and effort on your part? Or are they pie-in-the-sky things that are extremely unlikely to occur—ever?

One of the characteristics many happy people share is that they don't expect life to be perfect. And they're not sitting around waiting for that to happen either! They have the ability to do one of the following:

- Accept things as they are.
- Work to change events they don't like to a more acceptable level.
- Work around things they don't like.
- Leave an unworkable situation and find a new one.

So here's goal no. 5 – *Learn to be content with yourself and your situation.*

Please hear me. I am *not* suggesting you stay in a dangerous or unsafe situation. If you are in an abusive relationship, you need to *get out!* Get yourself (and children, if applicable) to a safe place, seek counsel, and see what needs to be done. God does not require anyone to be a punching bag and stay in a marriage where they are being regularly abused. Notice I'm not suggesting going to a divorce lawyer immediately—although to protect yourself and/or your children, it may come to that.

I'm talking about having realistic expectations for your life. If things have to be perfect in order for you to be happy, you're in for a pretty sad life. I like what Paul has to say:

> I am not saying this because I am in need, for I have learned to be content whatever the circumstances. I know what it is to be in need, and I know what it is to have plenty. I have learned the secret of being content in any and every situation, whether well fed or hungry, whether living in plenty or in want.
>
> Philippians 4:11–12 (NIV)

This is the attitude we all need to strive for—learning to enjoy and appreciate what we have and be content where we are. I'm not saying you should never try to change an undesirable situation. If you want a better job, a healthier body, or to travel more, go for it! But don't spend so much time wanting what you don't have that you miss what's right in front of you.

Another mistake people frequently make is comparing themselves with others. This is almost never a good idea. There will always be someone younger, richer, thinner, smarter, with more hair, etc., than you. Learn to enjoy what you have and who you are. The following poem is one of my favorites and has great advice. If more people took it to heart, the world would be a much happier place!

> If you compare yourself with others, you may become vain and bitter; for always there will be greater and lesser persons than yourself. Enjoy your achievements as well as your plans... Nurture strength of spirit to shield you in sudden misfortune. But do not distress yourself with

imaginings. Many fears are born of fatigue and loneliness... Therefore be at peace with God, whatever you conceive Him to be, and whatever your labors and aspirations, in the noisy confusion of life, keep peace in your soul. With all its sham, drudgery and broken dreams, it is still a beautiful world. Be cheerful. Strive to be happy.

Ehrmann, Max, "Desiderata," 1920.

Perfection Is Overrated

The last goal can be a little difficult to get across, and here it is.

Goal no. 7–Give yourself permission to not *be perfect.*

This really goes well with the poem in the last section ("Desiderata"). We live in a very productive society, and I often see people who have incredibly high standards of themselves and others. One of my pet peeves is hearing people tell their children, "Remember to just do your best." This sounds harmless and like a good thing, but is it?

Think about it. Is it a good idea to always try and do your best—at everything? Not so much, and I'll give an example to explain what I mean.

Let's say it's Saturday morning and you have a list of things you want to get done this weekend—something like the following.

- Mow the grass.
- Do laundry.
- Pay bills.
- Take the family to the zoo for a picnic.
- Go to church.
- Have a movie night with popcorn.

Pretty typical, right? How much time do you think the list will take to get done? Let's break it down to see.

- Mow the grass – three hours (medium-size lawn)
- Do laundry – three hours (two adults and two kids)
- Pay bills – thirty minutes
- Take the family to the zoo for a picnic – two to three hours
- Go to church – three hours (including Sunday school)
- Have a movie night with popcorn – three hours

I get about fifteen and a half hours—easily done in two days. However, what if you're a born–and-bred perfectionist and everything has to be done perfectly (remember, do your best!) in order for you to be able to cross it off your list and move on? If you're one of those people, it might take you six hours to mow the grass, seven hours to do laundry, two hours to pay bills, two hours just to get ready for the zoo, and by the time church and movie night roll around, the family is so stressed, no one wants to do them!

I'm trying to state this with some humor, but the sad thing is that a lot of people live pretty much exactly as I described in the above paragraph. Does this sound like much fun for them or their family? I can tell you the answer is a resounding *no!* I lived with just such a person for twenty-nine years, and none of us enjoyed it.

The point is that you don't have to be perfect all the time. People who are perfectionists are very black and white in their thinking and typically have two mental baskets that everything fits in—*perfect and terrible.* Anything that isn't perfect (almost everything) goes in the terrible basket. Can you see why these people are very seldom happy? They *live* in the terrible basket!

I'm proposing a third basket (which is mostly where I live, by the way) called *good enough.* Lots of things can be done good enough, and it's perfectly fine. Will anyone notice or care if you spend so much time working on your lawn that people could use it for a putting green? Does the laundry have to be starched, ironed, folded, and put away precisely? Not really. In my opinion, it's wasted time and effort! I always say that I want a perfectionist to be piloting any plane I'm flying on or performing any surgery on me. For most other things, good enough is completely satisfactory.

So learn to really manage your time well in a realistic manner. If you're getting ready to apply for a new job, you probably *do* want to spend a good amount of time on your resume and get to look as professional as possible. However, when you vacuum your floor, do you really need to get all the rows on the carpet to be parallel to each other and perfectly straight? (Yes, I know people who do this!)

Lighten up a bit and learn to save perfectionism for the areas where it really matters. For everything else, use the "good enough" basket and enjoy life more! Now let's take a look at how to manage the physical side of things.

Let's Get Physical

When someone is depressed, their tendency is to burrow into a deep, dark cave and seldom come out to see the light of day. I've encountered this over and over in depressed clients and friends. The blinds are tightly drawn, lights are off, the television and/or computer are on and often provide the only light source. If you're not already depressed when you walk into that kind of space, you will be after staying in it for a while! So here's your first goal:

Goal no. 1 – Improve your physical environment.

I've asked many depressed people over the years if retreating into a dark, closed-in space is helpful. At first I really thought some would say yes—after all, lots of unhappy people do it. The interesting thing is that over the years, I've never had *one* person tell me that sitting alone in the dark with no social contact is beneficial. So here's my approach now. Don't do it! If we know seclusion and retreat don't accomplish anything useful, there's no point in wasting time trying them. I realize that making an effort to step out of your comfort zone is tough, but let's face it, staying in your secure area isn't getting you any healthier either!

And let's talk about how comfortable your physical space really is. Does your home have clutter and stuff all over? Are there piles of clothes, shoes, books, magazines, laundry (dirty and clean), dishes, newspapers, bills, etc., lying everywhere? This is a tough one for me to be objective about because by nature I am extremely anti-clutter. My house looks lived in (especially when my two sons are home!) but it is neat and orderly. Things are picked up (mostly!), and more importantly, things have a place, so tidying up is relatively easy. It's just a matter of putting things back in their place after using them, not of *finding* a place to put them.

This tidiness didn't come easy because for twenty-eight years, I was married to the Clutter King. Ed never met anything he wanted to throw away. His battle cry was "We might need that someday!" So while he was alive, there were piles of stuff throughout our entire house. It was stressful, overwhelming, and disheartening. There wasn't much I could do about it except straighten the piles somewhat and look the other way.

I firmly believe the clutter added to Ed's depression and made our house *not* a sanctuary. After he was gone, I eventually cleaned out sixty-plus boxes of *stuff*—things that my sons and I decided *no one* would ever need anytime! For me the ultimate expression of Ed's unwillingness to part with useless objects was when I found a box full of packs of dispenser paper towels (ones that are used in medical and dental office bathrooms). The box was open, and the packs of paper towels were brown and crusty on the ends. I promptly determined that no one would ever need a box of grotty paper towels and threw them out, and told my sons that if it hadn't been for me, their father would have ended up on the TV show "Hoarders" one day!

I have observed that many of my depressed clients have homes that are overrun with clutter. The research I have done seems unclear on whether depression causes clutter or clutter causes depression, but I am convinced there is a connection. In fact, I feel so strongly about it that I frequently tell clients, "Clutter oppresses the spirit," and I believe it.

We live in a society that values having stuff and lots of it. You may have heard the expression, "He who dies with the most toys wins." I think that's symptomatic of our thinking. It's as if there's a contest to see who can collect the most things. Once we have the object we were so desperate to get, it frequently sits and gathers dust. We may not do much with our stuff, but by golly we have it!

So look around and be honest. Can you see your floors? How about your tabletops and countertops? I'm not saying there should be absolutely no clutter—then things would look almost sterile. But I strongly believe being surrounded by piles of things everywhere adds to stress and depression. So if your stuff is taking over your living space, it's time to de-clutter!

1–Now the hard part, *how to do it.* There are several options. I realize trying to sort through everything can be overwhelming. I frequently hear people say they don't even know where to start. If you can afford to, it might be easier to get some professional help. Look in the phone book or online for clutter busting or professional organizing. Getting a third party to come in will make things go much faster. Yes, you'll have to pay for their services, but the time you save, and the amount of space you'll clear up, may be worth it.

If hiring someone isn't financially possible and you think it's more than you can handle yourself, try an exchange with a friend (a well-organized friend!). Offer to mow their lawn, cook them some meals, or whatever you do well, if they'll help you get your mess under control.

If that's not an option either, you may be on your own. But don't despair—doing a "junk dump" (my term for it) isn't as hard as it sounds. The key is to start small and break the task down into little, manageable bites. You're not going to get your home organized in one day (especially if the mess has been months or years in the making). So here are the steps.

1. Get some trash bags, shopping bags, and boxes.
2. Pick something small to start on—a drawer, a dresser, or a closet (not a large master closet).
3. Empty everything out (yes, just dump it on the floor) and sort it into three piles:
   a. Keep.
   b. Give away or sell.
   c. Toss.

4. Put the toss pile directly into trash bags and haul out to the curb as soon as it's bagged up. Most neighborhoods have a big trash day once a month or so. If you have lots to throw out, you may need to leave your pile in the garage till then.

5. The giveaway pile needs to be boxed or bagged up and taken to your nearest charity. In some places, you can call different organizations (Salvation Army, Prevent Blindness, and others in my area). They'll come pick up your stuff and give you a tax receipt. I use these groups frequently.

   Note: If you think your giveaway items have some value, you might want to have a garage sale. A word of caution here: my experience is that garage sales are a *lot* of work and don't usually make that much money. People are looking for rock-bottom prices. If they can't find a good deal, they're not interested. (If you think something might be worth more than a few bucks, post it on Craigslist or eBay.) Your mentality at a garage sale has to be that people are paying *you* for the privilege of carrying off *your* junk. The objective is to see the stuff go away. Making any money is a bonus.

6. When deciding to keep something, ask yourself, "When was the last time I used this? Is this item in good shape?" (If it's ripped, stained, wrong size, or several years out of date, get rid of it.) Ask yourself, "If I keep this, even if it is in good shape, will I ever use it?" If the answer is no, toss it or give it away! Remember, even if something

is worthwhile and in good condition, if you're not going to ever use it, it's useless to *you*. Give it away and let someone else enjoy it.

7. Now that everything's sorted out, put back *only* the Keep pile. Arrange it nicely, step back, and admire your handiwork. If you're like me, you'll find reasons to go by the area you cleared out multiple times in the next few days to pat yourself on the back and enjoy how orderly everything looks.

8. Now put another organizing time on your calendar and do another drawer, dresser, bathroom, or closet. Once you get several chunks of real estate organized, you should have the confidence to move on to bigger and badder areas, like your garage or attic. Take it slowly and pace yourself. Don't spend all your free time taming clutter. Do a few areas and take a break—there's always next weekend. Set a goal to have X number of rooms done by X date and work toward that. What you'll find is the more you do, the better you feel, and the more motivated you are to do the rest. And as the clutter diminishes in your living space, the less oppressed and closed-in you'll feel—a good deal all the way around!

2–Once you get your space de-cluttered, the challenge is to keep it that way. So *get into the habit of tidying up your living space on a daily basis.* Mom had it right— you should make your bed every day! This is something I've done for years just because it makes me feel better than leaving the bed a mess. Now there's some research backing that up. Charles Duhigg says that making your bed every morning is linked to better productivity and stronger skills at sticking to a budget, and it boosts happiness. He calls making your bed a keystone habit, a practice that is a catalyst for other good behaviors. Keystone habits "help other habits to flourish by creating new structures, and they establish cultures where change becomes contagious," (Duhigg, Charles, *The Power of Habit, Why We Do What We Do in Life and Business*, New York: Random House, 2012).

WebMD states that bed makers are 19 percent more likely to report getting a good night's sleep on most days. "People reported sleeping longer hours and feeling better about going to bed when their bed was made, their sheets were fresh, and their bedroom was comfortable" ("Want to Sleep Better? Make Your Bed," WebMD, January 26, 2011 http://www.webmd.com/sleep-disorders/news/20110126/want-sleep-better-make-your-bed). I totally agree. There's just something very appealing about slipping into a neatly made bed vs. a rumpled, messy one. I also feel better when I walk through my bedroom during the day and see my pretty, neatly made bed. So take a few extra minutes in the morning and put your bed in order. It's worth the additional time and effort!

3–I discussed this in a previous section, but it's important, so I'll say it again. *Get some sunlight every day and don't live in a cave.* Dealing with depression by crawling back into your lair and having no contact with the outside world isn't helpful. So let the sunshine in! Open the curtains and windows and let some light and fresh air into your living space. You may feel dark inside, but there's no reason to make your living space murky and closed-in as well. When I walk into a gloomy, enclosed space, *I* feel sad, and I'm not prone to depression!

Therefore, put a little effort into improving your physical environment. After all, you probably spend a fair amount of time there, so it's worth your while to make it as pleasant as possible.

Take Care of Yourself

Depression has a huge impact on a person's physical health. The following is a list of some of the more common physical symptoms associated with depression.

- Headaches
- Back pain
- Agitation or restlessness
- Muscle aches and joint pain
- Chest pain
- Unexplained physical pain
- Reduced sex drive
- Digestive problems
- Exhaustion, loss of energy, and fatigue
- Sleeping problems
- Change in appetite or weight
- Dizziness or lightheadedness

It's a very circular phenomenon. Depression causes physical problems, and physical problems lead to depression. The best thing to do is to attempt to stop the negative downward spiral by inserting an improvement somewhere in the cycle. So your next objective is

Goal no. 2 – Improve your physical health.

Here are some things that might be helpful in this area.

1–I've seen over the years that depressed individuals appear to drag themselves through the day. They constantly feel exhausted and have no energy (lots of sleep doesn't seem to help). Because of this, they are prone to neglect daily habits such as personal grooming—I'm told it just takes too much effort. However, overlooking your individual sprucing up is not helpful. It just makes you feel more defeated and unhappy. It can also be unhealthy and cause a decline in your physical health (which then circles back and adds to your depression). So *get into (or back into) the habit of tidying yourself up.* Every day you should the following:

- Take a shower or bath, use soap, and put on deodorant.
- Change your clothes.
- Brush your teeth (at least twice a day, and floss three to four times a week).
- Use mouthwash.
- Comb or brush your hair.
- Wash your hands (especially before eating).
- Wash your face.

Once or twice a week, you should:

- Wash your hair.
- Clean and trim your finger and toenails.
- Shave your legs and underarms (women, unless you have a personal conviction against this).
- Shave your face (men, unless you're growing a beard or moustache).

On a regular basis—about once a month or every six weeks:

- Get a haircut.
- Trim your beard or moustache (men, this obviously depends on how fast your facial hair grows).

Some current research recommends showering or bathing every other day rather than every day. This is fine unless you regularly get sweaty or dirty. The point here is to make sure you *look* presentable to others and *feel* presentable to yourself. If you're having a down period, it doesn't help to look and feel like a mess. All that does is make you more depressed. So practice good personal grooming on a regular basis. It's worth the time spent.

2–Something that will help you look *and* feel better is to *get regular physical exercise.* This is something of a paradox for depressed individuals, however. Exercise requires planning and effort—both of which can be difficult to do if you're barely getting through the day. I realize this takes real effort, but the results are very much worth it. Numerous studies have been conducted looking at the effects of exercise on depression. Overall they tend to support the idea that regular exercise can decrease depression and improve general mood.

When you exercise, your body releases chemicals called endorphins. These endorphins reduce your perception of pain and trigger a positive feeling in the body, similar to that of morphine. Often people describe the feeling after a workout or run as euphoric. Runners frequently report a runner's high after a sprint. This tends to be associated with positive and energized feelings.

The good news is that you don't have to run a marathon to get the "feel good" effects of working out. I have run for years and really enjoy it. However, I have often thought that running really doesn't describe what I do; *plodding* comes much closer. I am a *very* slow runner. It's somewhat humiliating to admit, but there it is. I could feel bad about this, but I realized years ago that speed had nothing to do with how much I enjoy running. Whether I run a six-minute mile (never yet!) or twenty-minute mile, I still feel good when I'm finished.

So start off slow with something you know you can do. Try for three to four times per week in the beginning. Walking is a great way to start. Most of us know how to do it, and beyond comfortable shoes and clothes, no special equipment is needed. Don't stroll. Try to keep a brisk pace. Once you have walked for a couple of weeks, gradually increase your distance and try to decrease your time (so you're walking a little faster). Ironically, while I am the world's slowest runner, I am a pretty quick walker—go figure!

Then try adding other things. There are lots of exercises that can help decrease depression, if done on a regular basis. Here are a few:

- Aerobics
- Bicycling
- Dancing
- Gardening
- Golf (try to walk instead of using the cart)
- Lifting weights or strength training
- Jogging
- Playing tennis, basketball, or racquetball
- Rebounding (more about this below)
- Swimming
- Tai Chi
- Walking
- Yard work—digging, mowing, or raking
- Yoga

Rebounding is something I've done for years (and have recommended for clients) that not everyone is familiar with. It's basically bouncing up and down on a little trampoline. This doesn't sound like much, but read on! NASA states that exercise on a rebounder or mini-trampoline is "the most efficient and effective exercise yet devised by man." Rebounding is 68 percent more efficient than jogging (NASA, *Journal of Applied Physiology* 49(5): 881–887).

I usually do this in front of the television with a remote in one hand (I don't like commercials!). I run in place on it while watching TV. This is a great form of multitasking. Here are some of the benefits of this great little exercise:

- Fights fatigue
- Relieves joints and pain in the neck, back, and head
- Conditions and strengthens the heart
- Provides an extremely effective no-impact exercise
- Lowers elevated cholesterol and triglyceride levels
- Increases the performance of both the heart and the circulatory system
- Slows the aging process
- Stimulates the flow of lymph fluid through the lymphatic system
- Enhances digestion and relaxation
- Reduces blood pressure
- Improves coordination
- Improves sleep
- Reduces obesity

Can you see why this is considered a perfect exercise? I love it for several reasons:

- I can do it inside, so weather doesn't matter.
- I can rebound at home (I don't like having to go somewhere to work out).
- Rebounding is much easier on my joints than jogging on a solid surface.
- I can rebound while watching TV, so I'm distracted from the fact that I'm exercising!
- My rebounder is portable. I roll it out when I'm using it and then stand it up in my closet when I'm done.
- Rebounding can be done in a very small space. Even people living in a tiny apartment can rebound.
- Rebounders are very affordable. They will usually run from $50 to about $300.
- Rebounders are versatile. You can get folding ones with a carrying case to take with you when you travel. These tend to be the more expensive ones, but it you travel a lot, it may be worth it to you.

As you can see, rebounding is one of my favorite ways to exercise (and no, I'm not getting endorsements from any rebounder companies—sigh!). But if this doesn't sound like your thing, try something else. There was a big list of different ways to work out a few pages ago. Look through it and see if anything there sounds like a good possibility.

I recommend having more than one type of exercise to do. It's better for your body to mix it up some than just do the same workout all the time. So far today I have done a sixty-minute full-body workout video and jumped on my rebounder for about forty-five minutes. When I finish writing, I'll use a walk-in-place video and get in another forty to fifty minutes. I use weights during my full-body workout so that helps build muscle as well.

I'm going to make a few specific recommendations about tools that work well for me. If you're not familiar with the *Walk at Home* program, I suggest you look it up. Leslie Sansone started the WAH movement back in 1985, and it has been wildly popular ever since. I have about fifteen of her DVDs and use them regularly. They go from one to five miles. If you think walking isn't a real exercise, think again. I'm sweating when I finish some of the DVDs! I love these because they're easy to follow and can be done pretty much anywhere. When I travel, I always bring one or two with me. Her Web site is www.walkathome.com.

Another source I really like is www.beachbody.com. They have a *lot* of exercise DVDs, and I use several of them regularly. Ever heard of P90X? I don't use that one—too intense for me! I like the *Slim in 6* series with Debbie Siebers. These are several steps up from the Walk at Home in terms of intensity, so you may not want to start with these. I have all the Slim in 6 DVDs and try to do one five to six times a week. I rotate through them so I'm not doing the same one every time.

Please remember, these work for *me*—they may not be that great for *you*. Experiment some and see what you like. Before you invest any money, try borrowing DVDs or equipment from friends to see how it works. Walk at

Home has some free workouts you can try on their Web site, so you can get an idea of what they're about.

Try to get to the point where you're doing something physical every day for about twenty to thirty minutes a day—minimum! I know it takes a lot of effort, but the improvement in your looks, health, and mood will be well worth it!

3 – Cut out the cigarettes. If you are a smoker, now would be a great time to quit—yesterday would have been better! This is a terrific way to improve your physical health, and it may directly lessen your depression as well. Studies have consistently shown that smokers have a higher rate of depression than nonsmokers. Not only that, but smoking may directly *cause* depression. PsychCentral. com looks at various smoking/depression studies and states, "Evidence is consistent with the conclusion that there is a cause and effect relationship between smoking and depression in which cigarette smoking increases the risk of symptoms of depression" ("Depression and Smoking," Psych Central, accessed May 18, 2013, http:// psychcentral.com/library/depression_smoking.htm.)

As with all studies, this should be taken with a grain of salt. But even if there is no direct link between smoking and depression (and I believe there very well may be), we know that cigarette smoking impacts health negatively. For that reason alone, it's worth making the effort to quit. If you have smoked for several years, you may notice a positive difference very quickly after quitting. Your endurance will be better, food flavor will be improved, your clothes will smell cleaner, and you'll have more money in your pocket! So if you suffer from depression and you smoke, I encourage you to make efforts to quit. I believe it will be well worth it!

By the way, one of the most effective ways to quit smoking is through the use of hypnosis. I have used it for years with my clients and have had great results. I highly recommend this.

4 – *Cut down on alcohol.* Studies have found a strong link between serious alcohol use and depression. The big question is, does consuming alcohol on a regular basis lead to depression, or are depressed people more likely to drink excessively? There is research to support both sides of the issue. Nearly one-third of people with major depression also have an alcohol problem, according to a study conducted by the National Institute on Alcohol Abuse and Alcoholism ("Alcohol and Depression." WebMD, accessed May 20, 2013. http://psychcentral.com/library/depression_smoking.htm.).

I have nothing against someone having a glass of wine or a beer. In fact, in very small amounts, alcohol can help a person feel more relaxed or less anxious. However, depressed people often drink heavily in an attempt to feel better about their situation. This almost never works, mostly because alcohol is a *depressant*, which means it slows the function of the central nervous system. Alcohol blocks some of the messages trying to get to the brain. This alters a person's perceptions, emotions, movement, vision, and hearing.

So if you are prone to depression, watch your alcohol levels. Drinking to feel better is truly not a good idea. There are many other better ways to achieve that effect.

Adding a drinking habit on top of your depression is an excellent way to increase your depression level.

5 – This will be a short section because the piece of advice *don't use drugs* has a lot in common with the one above, cutting down on alcohol. Really, everything I said about why drinking heavily is a bad idea and doesn't help your depression level applies (in some cases, even more!) to using drugs. So I'm not going to belabor the point. Just remember that dosing yourself on chemicals will likely only intensify your depression, not make it go away.

6 – *Eat a balanced diet.* There is a *lot* of research on the link between depression and nutrition. Most of it agrees on a few key points, namely that people who are depressed may tend to

- eat a lot of junk and/or processed food,
- crave sweets
- eat too much or skip meals altogether,
- not get enough of certain vitamins—mainly B and D.

There are a myriad of diets out there. Be careful in following one because a lot of them are fads and not really healthy. I'm going to list several that I believe are well balanced and will promote good physical and emotional health.

- *American Heart Association* – They have some good dietary suggestions on their Web site.
- *American Diabetes Association* – Ditto above.
- *Weight Watchers* – They have a healthy, well-rounded food plan. This can also be used to lose weight if this is your goal.

Any of these can be helpful and will have you eating nutritious, well-balanced meals. I would be wary of any program that has you eating or drinking food supplements instead of real food. Also, realize that many of the weight loss programs want you to buy some type of pill that will supposedly help you be healthier and lose weight. Some of them may actually live up to their claims, but I suspect most don't. Check out any program you are interested in thoroughly before signing on. The main things to remember in terms of food and depression are the following:

- Watch the junk/processed food.
- Limit your alcohol.
- Eat more fruits and vegetables.
- Eat fish a few times a week.

A note on food shopping. Many of us go for convenience and have a lot of processed foods in our home. Start at the very beginning of the eating process and make a habit of *shopping* correctly. I love stores like Whole Foods, Sprouts, and local Farmer's Markets. They have healthy foods attractively displayed (with fun food samples!). I planned weekly menus for years when my boys were growing up. (I don't anymore because I just cook for one.) It wasn't anything fancy. I just got a piece of paper and wrote out what we would eat for dinner each night. It looked something like this:

Monday – Pot roast with potatoes and carrots
Tuesday – Hamburger patties, french fries, salad
Wednesday – Tuna casserole, green beans
Thursday – Homemade pizza, salad
Friday – Brisket, rice, peas
Saturday – Taco salad
Sunday – Spaghetti and meatballs, bread, salad

The beauty of having a menu is that I knew what I needed to get at the grocery store. The menu was my guideline for shopping, and it accomplished another important function—we didn't eat the same thing all the time. For several years I had a list of about three weeks worth of meals posted on the refrigerator. When I was stumped on what to have a certain day, I would look at my list and pick a meal from it. In case you were wondering, everything on the above menu was homemade (I cook and bake). It's much healthier and cheaper that way, and it tastes better!

If you're kitchen challenged, don't worry. There are things that can help that. And I confess, I'm no gourmet chef. My cooking was pretty simple, but it did the job. One thing that was very helpful for me was taking cooking classes periodically. I took some Italian cooking courses early in my marriage and learned to make spaghetti sauce, meatballs, pizza sauce, pizza dough, and Italian sausage all from scratch. It was fun and easy, and those classes more than paid for themselves over the years. So look for some cooking classes in your area and sign up.

I've also seen places that help you assemble ingredients for meals, package them up, and take them home with cooking instructions. They have all the ingredients and usually have a list of meals to choose from. Once you get the food components home, you can freeze them till you need them. This can be a fun activity for the whole family. Working together for a few hours can produce ready-to-assemble meals for several weeks.

However you do it, find a plan that works for you and start following it. Make it a point to eat fresh, healthy food and try cooking more yourself. You don't have to be isolated in the kitchen either. Involve your family and make food preparation and dinner a family affair. I think you'll like the results!

7 – The last tip in improving your physical health is *get a good night's sleep*. Interestingly enough, this is an area that can go either way. Depressed individuals tend to sleep either too much or not enough. According to Patrick McNamara, "It has been known for some time that there is a strong relation between sleep and depression. When we get depressed we sleep too much or too little and we wake up too early in the morning. We never feel totally refreshed by sleep and sleep, when it comes, is fitful and punctuated by too many awakenings. I know of no cases of depression without profound disruption of sleep" ("Dream Catcher–The Neuroscience of Our Night Life," *Psychology Today*, accessed May 21, 2013, http://www.psychologytoday.com/blog/dream-catcher/201107/sleep-and-depression.)

Here are some facts on sleep and depression from the National Sleep Foundation.

("Depression and Sleep," accessed May 22, 2013, http://www.sleepfoundation.org/article/sleep-topics/depression-and-sleep)

- Among adolescents who reported being unhappy, 73 percent reported not sleeping enough at night.
- Insomnia is very common among depressed patients.
- Sleep problems are associated with more severe depressive illness.
- Depression may cause sleep problems, and sleep problems may cause or contribute to depressive disorders.

So how much sleep is desirable? Again, here is what the National Sleep Foundation recommends.

Newborns (0–2 months)	12–18 hours
Infants (3–11 months)	14–15 hours
Toddlers (1–3 years)	12–14 hours
Preschoolers (3–5 years)	11–13 hours
School-age children (5–10 years)	10–11 hours
Teens (10–17)	8.5–9.25 hours
Adults	7–9 hours

I'm not going to focus on depressed individuals who get too much sleep here. That solution is simpler. Start doing things to combat the depression and begin limiting the amount of sleep you get. (Notice I said *simpler*, not necessarily *simple*). I'm going to look at the unhappy individuals who are chronically short on slumber.

I have believed for years that this is a severe problem in our country. We are a nation of walking sleep-deprived people! Somehow we have gotten the notion that eight hours of sleep a night is nice from time to time but not really a necessity. This is a huge mistake. I've listed below some of the results of chronic insomnia:

- More susceptibility to infections and longer healing times
- Deficits in memory and attention
- Higher probability of accidents—some severe
- Eating and weighing more
- Higher blood pressure
- Higher rate of inactivity
- Higher levels of irritability
- Decreased performance and alertness
- Relationship problems
- Decreased quality of life
- Decreased sex drive

And of course, there is the effect that is the topic of this book—increased rates of depression. WebMd states, "In a 2007 study of 10,000 people, those with insomnia were five times as likely to develop depression as those without. In fact, insomnia is often one of the first symptoms of depression. Insomnia and depression feed on each other. Sleep loss often aggravates the symptoms of depression, and depression can make it more difficult to fall asleep" ("Coping With Excessive Sleepiness–10 Things to Hate About Sleep Loss," WedMD, accessed May 20, 2013. http://www.webmd.com/sleep-disorders/ excessive-sleepiness-10/10-results-sleep-loss).

So what can you do to increase your chances of getting a good night's sleep? So glad you asked, and here are some suggestions.

- *Listen to some soothing music designed for relaxation.* New age music can be a good choice. This is an umbrella term for various down-tempo music intended to create artistic inspiration, relaxation, and optimism. It is used by listeners for yoga, massage, meditation, and reading as a method of stress management or to create a peaceful atmosphere in their home or other environments (definition from Wikipedia). I have several CDs of it, and I play it almost constantly in counseling and hypnosis sessions.
- While I am a huge advocate of exercise, *stop working out about 2–3 hours before you plan on going to bed.*
- *Don't eat a heavy meal shortly before turning in.* This makes it difficult to get comfortable enough to sleep well and can also cause acid reflux.
- *Watch your technology use.* Turn off your cell phone, television, computer, and tablet about an hour before going to sleep. Ed was notorious for leaving the television on *all* night. I tried to convince him that this was a bad idea, but he had suffered from

insomnia most of his life and had developed this unhealthy habit. (Research shows that I'm right about this, by the way.)

- *Create a relaxing bedtime routine.* I have been telling clients this for years. Many of us do this instinctively for our children but not for ourselves. Dim the lights, play soft music, take a warm bath, read a book, or have a cup/glass of herbal tea. (Chamomile, lavender, and kava-kava all aid relaxation. There are some specifically blended to help you unwind. I believe Celestial Seasoning has a blend called Sleepytime).

- *Reserve the bedroom exclusively for sleeping.* I had a client recently tell me that she and her husband regularly have their biggest fights in the bedroom. They go there so their children won't hear them. It's good to shield your children from arguments, but associating fighting with the bedroom does *not* make that a relaxing place. Don't use your bedroom as an office either. Working on your taxes in bed makes it difficult to unwind there later.

- *Add a soothing noise source*—to block other, less soothing noises. I have slept for years with a little round white machine in my room called a White Noise Maker. They're available online for about $50. Mine is adjustable, and it emits a constant, soothing noise, like a fan but without the breeze. Now both of my sons use them as well. I highly recommend them.

- *Make sure your bed is comfortable.* It's worth spending some money to ensure this. Remember, you're investing in your health. Have comfortable pillows and good quality sheets. If you can't afford a new mattress, invest in a well-made mattress topper. I have a memory foam mattress topper on my bed. It's worth every penny I paid for it! I also splurged on 800 count Egyptian cotton sheets (on sale half price), and they're wonderful. It feels almost decadent sliding into bed! And make your bed every morning. There's just something appealing about slipping into a neatly made, attractive, and comfortable bed at the end of the day.

- *Learn some relaxation techniques.* These can be pretty simple—deep breathing, counting backward from 100, reciting the alphabet backward, etc. Anything that will ease your mind and help you gently unwind.

- *Watch your caffeine, alcohol, and sugar use in the evenings.* I learned years ago that if I had caffeine or sugar too late in the day, I would pay for it with a sleepless night. So if I must have a really rich dessert, I try to eat it at lunch, so it has several hours to work its way out of my system. At home I always drink herbal tea, and that takes care of the caffeine. But sometimes when I'm eating dinner out, I forget and order iced tea at a restaurant. Several hours later I realize what I've done (it was regular, caffeinated tea), and I'll usually be awake for hours.

- *Adjust the room temperature.* Most people sleep better in a cool room rather than a warm one.

- *Try to make your bedroom as dark as possible while you're sleeping.* Again, most of us sleep better that way. Try to block even little bits of light, such as the light on your DVR. The American Medical Association issued a policy recognizing "that exposure to excessive light at night, including extended use of various electronic media, can disrupt sleep or exacerbate sleep disorders, especially in children and adolescents." Those little blue lights on your computers and TVs can be very detrimental to a good night's sleep. Try to cover them up to improve your chance of getting some zzzz's.

Decide to De-stress

The next area is one most of us struggle with and could use some help overcoming:

Goal no. 3 – Decrease your stress levels.

We all have demanding areas in our lives—difficult family members, demanding bosses, hectic lifestyles, and not enough hours in the day to get everything done. Most of us suffer from the common malady of having not enough time or resources to meet the demands placed on us. Therefore, our stress levels can go through the roof. I wrote about this a bit in the "Things That Can Help – Emotional" section, and I'll go into more depth here.

1 – Here's the thing to remember. When you're in a tense situation, you have two choices:

- Change the stressful *situation.*
- Change your *response* to the stressful situation.

The first one is pretty self-explanatory, although not always easy to execute. And please be aware that most of these changes cannot be made quickly. These situations may take weeks to months to fully alter. Some examples of circumstances you could change are listed below.

- Getting out of a negative relationship
- Quitting a financially rewarding but emotionally draining job
- Going back to school to learn a new set of skills (in order to eventually get a better job)
- Moving out of your current living place to escape a demanding roommate (or getting the roommate to move out of your place)

There are some other possible ways to directly affect the state of affairs, and I'll give some specific examples.

- *Try avoiding the situation so you don't encounter the person or event.* Walk your dog at a different time of day in order to dodge your obnoxious neighbor, drive a different way to work and see if the traffic is any better, or give yourself permission not to answer the phone when you see that your cousin who takes advantage of you is calling (let it go to voice mail and check it—if it's important, you can always call back).
- *Give yourself a break.* If work is becoming overwhelming, get up and walk around some, just to get a change of scenery. Hand deliver something instead of e-mailing—sometimes physically moving around helps you feel better.

Make a deal with yourself to get X amount of work done on cleaning out your attic and then going to see a movie with friends.

- *Insert a change into your routine.* Often just looking at things from a different perspective gives stress relief and new insight. If you're anxious and unhappy because you're still single and would really like to be in a relationship, try some new things that might help. Initiate a dinner party and invite friends you haven't seen in a while, try a new health club instead of the one you've always gone to, visit some other churches in your area and check out the singles groups, etc.

If you can't actually change the stressful situation, try improving it. One of the following often helps:

- *Listen to soothing music.* Certain types of music are *not* calming to me, and if I'm exposed to them for long, I can feel my stress level rising. If you work in a place where you're subjected to music you find annoying, ask *nicely* if the listener will wear headphones.
- *Get some aromatherapy going.* I love the scents of vanilla and baby powder—they always soothe me.
- *The sound of water moving is almost universally de-stressing.* Get a small tabletop fountain and turn it on. You can find them online for under $100.

If changing the situation is possible, great! This may be all you need to do to significantly improve things. However, often changing the situation is simply not feasible. That's when we move to the second choice—changing your response.

This is a very important coping skill to acquire because there are *lots* of things in life we have no control over, and they can be incredibly annoying! When we encounter one, we can choose to become stressed, angry, frustrated, etc., *or* we can pick a different way to react.

I'll give an example from my own life. I taught at Mid-American Christian University for four years. I loved what I did, and the students and the people I worked with were great. There was one thing about the job that I didn't like however—the drive back and forth. I lived in north Oklahoma City at the time, almost in Edmond. MACU is located in south OKC, practically in Moore. I discovered that when I left right at 7:00 a.m., the drive took twenty-five to thirty minutes. However, if I left any later than 7:25 a.m., the drive took forty-five to fifty minutes and was in heavy traffic all the way.

The solution I came up with was to leave every morning at 7:00 a.m. This was not ideal because it meant I had to wake up at 5:30 a.m. in order to get out the door on time. I wasn't fond of that part, but after fighting the traffic and arriving at school with my nerves completely frazzled a few times, I decided that getting up early was the lesser of two evils. This meant that I was one of the first ones there, had plenty of time to get settled in, and could start teaching in a calm, peaceful frame of mind. An added bonus was that I was always able to nab a great parking space!

To me this is a commonsense approach, and I don't understand why more people don't do it. I frequently see people stuck because they want things to change *for them*. I would love that too, but I happen to have a very practical, realistic mind-set, and I realize the world doesn't revolve around me. Many times I would like it to, but so far it hasn't happened.

So if you are in a challenging situation that is causing you significant stress, take a realistic look at it. Do some brainstorming alone or with a friend. Can anything about the issue be changed or modified? If so, would that make things better for you? Here's the rule of thumb I've been telling clients for years. If two or more people are in a situation and one of them is unhappy with it, the person who is the most unhappy is usually the one who needs to change it.

What I invariably hear after making this comment is, "But that's not fair! They're the one causing the problem, why should I be the one to change?" That's a reasonable question with a simple answer. Since the situation appears to be working for them (although sometimes not very well), they have no motivation to change. You're the one who's displeased with things, so you'll need to be the one to try and transform them.

Change is hard and lots of work. Usually we don't even attempt it unless we're highly motivated to do so. Let me give some common examples of instances where *we* might have to be the ones to change even though *someone else* is causing the problem.

- Your neighbor's dog barks its head off every time someone walks by their house.
- Your dear friend or significant other has a bad habit of interrupting you whenever you talk.

- Your coworker drops into your office frequently and stays to chat for lengthy periods of time, making it difficult to get any work done.

Think about each of these scenarios. Is the other person apt to change unless you say something? It seems unlikely to me, so if you want things to be different, the ball may be in your court. A good place to start with each of these examples is to talk to the other person. Think about what you want to say and jot down your major points on an index card. That way you don't forget them in the heat of the moment. If this is too uncomfortable for you, try sending them an e-mail. Keep it short, friendly, and to the point. Two to three paragraphs should be plenty.

If that doesn't do the trick, move on to the next level. With your neighbor you may need to involve your neighborhood association—or the city where you live. There may be laws that are being violated. With your coworker, you might need to pull in your supervisor or the HR department. If your friend or significant other is not responsive, it's tougher. The best bet is to *respond differently* if they keep interrupting. Say firmly but pleasantly, "Please wait until I finish. I promise I'll give you plenty of time to talk, and I'll listen while you do." If they're afraid they'll forget what they wanted to say (Ed used this excuse with me), give them a pad of paper and pen. They can jot their point down and bring it up when it's their turn. Unfortunately, if you don't change your response, they're unlikely to change theirs. And please note, you'll probably need to be the one to start the process, *and* you'll likely need to repeat it several times before they get the message.

2–*Learn some relaxation techniques.* I've talked about this in a couple of other sections, but it bears repeating. The saying is, manage your stress, or your stress will manage you. I don't know who first said it, but it's absolutely correct. Let me give you some stats on stress (American Psychological Association, Stress in America Findings, 2010). The following were the top concerns:

- Money (76 percent)
- Work (70 percent)
- The economy (65 percent)
- Family responsibilities (58 percent)
- Relationships (55 percent)
- Personal health concerns (52 percent)
- Housing costs (52 percent)
- Job stability (49 percent)
- Health problems affecting my family (47 percent)
- Personal safety (30 percent)

While one-third of parents felt under pressure, and 69 percent stated managing stress is important, only 32 percent felt they were doing a good job at it. Stress also has behavioral consequences, which, in excess, could have physical consequences.

- Two-fifths of adults reported overeating or eating unhealthy foods because of stress in the past month.
- Nearly one-third said they skipped a meal because of stress in the past month.

- More than four in ten said they had lain awake at night in the past month.
- The most common physical symptoms of stress reported were irritability (45 percent), fatigue (41 percent), and lack of energy or motivation (38 percent).

  (Stress in America: Our Health at Risk, January 11, 2012)

I've said this over and over to clients—unmanaged stress has very real negative consequences. So if you're feeling pressured and tense (and who isn't!), try some of the following to get things better under control.

- *Deep breathing* – one of the easiest techniques to master. I went into this in depth in the, "Things That Can Help – Mental" section so please refer to that.
- *Exercise* – Yes, that dreaded word. I've addressed this in several places, so I won't go into it again.
- *Take a timeout* – I just took a snack, my book, and glass of iced tea and went out to my back patio. I took a short eating and reading break and felt better afterward!
- *Connect with others* – When is the last time you got together with your friends and went out to eat, to a concert, to a movie, etc.? If you can't remember, it's been too long!
- *Journal* – This is a very effective way of processing stress.
- *Meditate* – This is a great way to de-stress, and it's very scriptural (Joshua 1:8, Psalm 19:14, Psalm

119:5, and Psalm 1:1–6 along with many others address this topic).

- *Take a hike* – Go outside and walk around for twenty to thirty minutes. You get exercise, natural light, and a change of scenery all in one.
- *Practice self-hypnosis* – This sounds difficult but is actually fairly easy. Figure out what you want to change and write out five to six instructions about it. As you're lying in bed, repeat them slowly to yourself (silently, you don't want to disturb your spouse) until you fall asleep. Things like, I will exercise at least once a day, I will eat more fruits and vegetables, I will walk away when my coworker starts annoying me, I will think before I speak, etc.

There are lots of different ways to cope better with stress. Start trying some, and if one doesn't work, pick another method. Make up a list of what is effective for you so you can use it again. Get into the habit of doing something to lower your stress on a regular basis—several times a week to several times a day. It will be worth the time and effort.

3 – *Learn to have fun again*—also addressed previously. This is one of my favorite recommendations to make. A client told me one time, "I'm going to tell my husband that my doctor said I should go get a pedicure regularly." Absolutely!

Do something fun at least on a weekly basis, something just for you. Kids do this naturally, but we lose it as we grow older. Having a sense of enjoyment about our daily lives is a great way of keeping things in perspective. I believe, and have preached for years, that participating in pleasurable activities lowers our stress levels, keeps us balanced, and gives zest to life. Here are some recommendations on how to do this.

- *Develop a sense of humor.* Watch funny movies or television shows, acquire a repertoire of jokes, and keep an eye out for the ridiculous—I promise it's out there! Be aware, however, that there is a difference between humor and sarcasm.
- *Get into the habit of smiling.* This can be very contagious, it costs nothing, and you'll feel happier and lighter.
- *Acquire a sense of curiosity.* Ever notice how many questions children ask? That's because the world is a place of wonder to them. Get some of that freshness back into your life.
- *Try something new.* I know I've said this a lot, but as adults, most of us develop routines that we seldom deviate from. So break free and sit in a different spot in church, walk a different route in your neighborhood, resolve to try one new restaurant a month, etc.
- *Have a "no TV" night with your family and break out the board games or a jigsaw puzzle.* We did this regularly growing up, and Ed and I did it some with David and Josh. The kids will love it, and you'll be surprised at how much you actually connect with each other.
- *Slow it down!* Do you rush through your days and try to cram a whole list of activities in it? (I must

admit, I'm guilty of this one). Give yourself a few hours a week to just relax. Lately I've gotten in the habit of taking a long bubble bath on Saturday night—just me, my glass of iced tea, and a magazine. I feel very pampered and relaxed when I'm done.

- *Remember to play now and then.* Put time in your schedule to do things that are *not* productive, just fun. Go for a bike ride with your family, read a story to your kids, have a Chinese fire drill at the stoplight, read a new book, try a new recipe, do an art project, rearrange the furniture, check out some garage sales, go geocaching, bake some cookies, have a picnic at the zoo, eat dinner outside—get the picture?

Having fun is not a silly indulgence—far from it! Fun is a way of restoring balance and perspective, it reduces stress and anxiety, and it makes us feel more connected to other. So on a regular basis, slow it down and take a fun break. You'll feel better for it!

4 – Often when we're stressed and depressed, the focus is squarely on us. It's all about our difficulties, issues, concerns, etc. So it can be very helpful to get a change of perspective. A great way to do this is to *help someone else.* This takes the focus off you and your problems. A sad fact of life is that if we look around, we'll almost always find someone who is worse off than we are. That can be a very sobering realization.

Get into the habit of helping others out. This can be done with friends and family or with total strangers.

There are lots of very worthy organizations who would love some help—Habit for Humanity, Salvation Army (be a bell ringer!), Red Cross, etc. You can also pick out some local groups to assist: hospitals, churches, schools, soup kitchens—take your pick. Years ago I knew a couple who went to our church faithfully every week and spent a few hours folding bulletins for the Sunday service (this was before folding machines). It was a small thing, but it needed to be done and allowed the staff to do other things.

The home makeover shows are extremely popular (and I love them!), but we don't have to go quite that large scale to be effective. Here are some doable options that are smaller but still helpful.

- When you're getting ready to run errands, call a neighbor who has small children or who has been sick and offer to get some things for them.
- Offer a babysitting evening to some friends who are having a rough time so they can have a few hours away.
- Take a friend who has been having difficulties out to lunch. Make it a priority to listen to them rather than do most of the talking yourself.
- Write a letter to a friend or family member who has recently lost someone. Share a memory you have about the person who passed away—it can be funny or serious.
- I had a friend who used to see people asking for money on the streets. He would head for the nearest fast-food place and buy them a meal and take it to them. This is much better than giving them money, by the way.

- Volunteer to be a Big Brother, Big Sister, scout leader, Sunday School teacher, teacher assistant at your local school or anything else that helps kids.

As you can see, there are lots of options. The point is to take the focus off yourself periodically. People who are depressed easily develop tunnel vision and only see themselves and their issues. It can be very helpful to remind yourself that other people have problems too, and assisting others can be very rewarding. I like the following poem by Calvin Coolidge that really states this well.

Thoroughbred Code

I believe in work,
For discontent and labor are not often companions.
I believe in thrift,
For to store up a little regularly is to store up character
    as well.
I believe in simple living,
For simplicity means health and health means happiness.
I believe in loyalty,
For if I am not true to others, I cannot be true to myself.
I believe in holding up my chin,
For self-respect commands respect from others.
I believe in keeping up the courage,
For troubles flee before a brave front.
I believe in bracing up my brother,
For an encouraging word may save the day for him.
I believe in living up to that best that is in me,
For to lower the standard is to give up the fight.

Be Positively Proactive

One of the worst things about depression, in my opinion, is that it's so enervating. It can completely drain all the energy, drive, creativity, optimism, motivation, and get-up-and-go out of a person. As I've said before, the perfect description of a depressed person is one who sits in a dark room staring at a blank wall. Even the thought of trying to get up and do something can be exhausting.

Because of that, I realize this next goal is not going to come naturally, to say the least. But it is very necessary if you want to get better.

Goal no. 4 – Have some concrete goals to work toward.

1 – *A good antidepression technique is to find something productive to do and work hard at it.* The problem with doing what feels right in depression is that *nothing* feels right. And doing nothing eventually makes you feel even worse. The thing to remember here is that depression

sets up what we call in counseling a negative downward spiral. I referred to this earlier in the book, and what this means is, a series of thoughts or actions that feeds back to itself, causing a situation to become progressively worse over time.

Depressed individuals pretty much *live* in negative downward spirals. Let me give you an example of how these work.

Mark is feeling down because he had a run-in with his boss at work. Since Mark is prone to depression, he has been telling himself what an idiot he is to have messed up the project he was working on, even though his boss only asked him to correct a few minor points. On the way home, an impatient driver behind him leans angrily on his horn and makes an obscene gesture when he passes Mark's car. Mark tells himself that the other driver has it in for him.

When Mark arrives at home, his family is getting ready to go to daughter Sara's soccer game. His wife Laura cheerfully tells Mark to hurry up and change because they need to leave in ten minutes. Mark had forgotten about the game and feels defensive about it, so he replies angrily to Laura's comment. He feels terrible about Laura's hurt look; however, he can't bring himself to explain and apologize, so he and Laura spend the game carefully not speaking to each other. Laura talks with several other parents and is able to have a good time. A few people try to strike up a conversation with Mark but are met with glum silence so quickly leave him alone.

When the game is over, several parents suggest taking the kids to a local pizza place for dinner. Mark makes an excuse not to go, and in the rush to get off the ball park, the other parents take his excuse at face value, and no one presses him to join them. Mark returns to an empty, silent house with the following messages replaying over and over in his head:

I'm so stupid. I completely messed up the project at work. My boss thinks I'm an idiot. He'll probably fire me as soon as he can. Even people on the freeway think I'm a loser. They all treat me like that joker did earlier today. I'm also a rotten father and husband. What kind of person forgets about his kid's soccer game and then snaps at his wife for no reason? And obviously the other parents don't like me, no one talked to me at the game, and no one cared that I didn't go eat with them.

Mark is putting the worst possible interpretations on the events of his day—notice there is no giving the benefit of doubt. Everything that happened to him is terrible and, at least in his mind, is all because he is such a bad, unworthy, undeserving person. So every message he gives himself sends him further down that negative downward spiral, and consequently, he feels worse and worse. When his family comes home, Mark is, you guessed it, sitting in the living room staring at the wall.

One of the best antidotes to depression is to take some type of action. And it's best if the action is organized and purposeful. So let's suppose Mark gets home, takes a few deep breaths, and addresses his day differently. Instead of the above messages, let's say he tries something like the following:

Okay, I messed up a few minor points on the presentation, but the boss said that the rest was really well done. I'll fix the spots he talked to me about this weekend. It should only take an hour or so. And that guy on the freeway, who knows what was going on with him. Maybe his day was worse than mine! I'm not going to take that personally. He was just an impatient driver who would have honked at anyone who got in his way. I feel bad about forgetting Sara's game, and I shouldn't have snapped at Laura. I'll apologize to both of them when they get back. And I really can't blame the other parents for not talking to me much tonight—a few of them tried, and I didn't give them the slightest bit of encouragement. I wouldn't have talked to me either!

Great. The self-talk is taken care of. After some more thought, Mark decides to put some things on his to-do list for the weekend so he'll get some things accomplished. He starts things off by going through his clothes and collecting several bags of things that can be given away, something Laura has been asking him to do. When his family gets home, he goes out to welcome them cheerfully. He commends Sara on the game she played and greets Laura with a kiss and an apology. Later on he tells Laura about his day and shows her the list he's started for the weekend. She is thrilled to see that he's gone through his clothes, and together, they add a few more items to the to-do list, including a movie for the entire family. When Monday morning arrives, Mark is feeling rested, upbeat, and energized. He and Laura accomplished several things around the house and did some fun family activities as well.

Does Mark sound familiar to you? We all fall into this behavior at times. The trick is to recognize it and pull ourselves out when we're there. If you feel aimless and adrift (as well as depressed or anxious), positive, organized action can be a great remedy. Look at your life situation. What are some things you see that could be improved? Often you can get a good idea of this by simply walking around your house and yard. Make a list of things that need to be done. Your list might have things like the following:

- Clean out the refrigerator.
- Fix the steps on the back deck.
- Finish putting up the back fence.
- Paint the railing on the front porch.
- Plant some flowers and shrubs.

We all have (or should have!) a list of things that need to be done. If you can't think of any, you can come by my house! It is true, however, that we don't always see items that are right in front of us. If you really can't find anything that needs to be fixed, painted, planted, cleaned, or moved, ask a family member or friend. I'm sure they will find several things for you to work on. The great part is that once you start working on your list and are able to cross items off, you have a feeling of pride, accomplishment, and satisfaction. None of these are conducive to depression!

2 – The next part fits in so well with the above that there's a fair amount of overlap, but I decided to list them separately anyway. *Do a positive construction (or positive action) at least once a day*, something (preferable tangible) that you can look back at later and feel good about doing.

It may seem like I'm belaboring the point here, but depressed individuals are notorious for living in their heads. They overthink most things and then get stuck because they've developed paralysis of analysis. Nothing ever gets done, and then they feel worse! So getting up and moving is critical for overcoming depression. And it doesn't have to be a huge task. Lots of small ones will work just as well. Remember, enough baby steps will take you a long way! The following is a list of possible positive constructions.

- Weed a flower bed.
- Wash your car.
- Have lunch with a friend.
- Organize a drawer or drawers.
- Mow the grass for your older neighbor.
- Clean your grill.
- Take your family and dog to the lake or beach.
- Bake some cupcakes for your family and share them with a friend.
- Work on a hobby.
- Send someone a note of thanks or appreciation
- Try a new restaurant.
- Play a game with your child.

The possibilities are truly endless, and there's no right or wrong way to do this. The point here is to take action and not let depression keep you stuck. With depression typically, the *less* you do, the *worse* you feel, and the *more* you do, the *better* you feel. We'll look next at the last section—"Things That Can Help – Spiritual."

Connect With Your Creator

We've looked at things that can help manage and control depression in the emotional, mental, and physical areas. But there is one more important sphere we need to examine, the spiritual aspect. In my opinion, this is the most vital and is often the part that is neglected.

In order to live a fulfilled, happy, and productive life, we need to accomplish the following:

Goal no. 1 – Make ourselves right with God.

God created the world and everything in it, and it was wonderful beyond our capacity to imagine it. But Satan was jealous of God's marvelous creation and started doings things to corrupt it. (Satan, by the way, is *not* God's equal. He is a fallen angel who is, in every way, inferior to God.) So we were all born into a fallen, sinful world.

This sin had many serious and far-reaching consequences. The most crucial was that it separated us from God. So we were lost and hopeless because there was no way we could reach God in our own strength. The penalty for sin is death. We were all doomed to eternal separation from God, which is the definition of hell.

God saw our plight and decided to make a way for us to come to him. He sent his own son to die in *our* place for *our* sins. This was done at an unimaginable cost to both God and his son. Jesus died on the cross in our place with the weight of all our sins on his shoulders. He did this willingly so that we might have a way to salvation.

But wait, the best part of this story is that he didn't stay dead. After three days, his tomb was empty because he was alive! He defeated death and gave us hope of eternal life, shared with him in heaven. And here's the really unbelievable part. All we have to do to get this eternal life is ask for it. It's that simple. We tell God we realize we were sinners and are sorry for that. Then we thank him for the gift of his son's death and resurrection. And we accept it. Yes, just like that.

If you have not done this, there is nothing more important that you need to take care of. I hope you will take a minute and recite the following prayer:

> Dear Lord Jesus,
>
> I know that I am a sinner, and I ask for your forgiveness. I believe you died for my sins and rose from the dead. I turn from my sins and invite you to come into my heart and life. I want to trust and follow you as my Lord and Savior. In your name. Amen.
>
> (Billy Graham – The Sinner's Prayer)

At the moment we utter that prayer, God receives us into his family. We become his precious son or daughter, and we have *lots* of brothers and sisters all over the world. Becoming a Christian (that's what it's called) does not mean that our lives will be perfect from now on—I wish! What it does mean is that we have an amazing set of resources we can use to deal with life's problems and difficulties. Being a child of God is just like being a physical child—there's continual growth involved. More about that later. First, I want to address a few other issues.

There are two points people seem to get hung up on over Christianity:

1. There should be more than one way to God.
2. Christianity is exclusive and keeps lots of people out.

Neither statement is true, and I'll discuss them both now. I'm always amazed that people put so much energy into demanding multiple ways to get to God and saying they should all be equally valid. Here's how I visualize this.

Picture yourself out hiking in some very tall mountains. You want to continue in the direction you're heading in (we'll say north) but abruptly you come to a huge gorge. This thing is so deep you literally can't see the bottom; you see clouds floating far *underneath* where you're standing! You look around for a way to get across, but you don't see one, and there's nothing lying around you can use to build something to help you get to the other side. You feel despair because you know there's no way you can cross over by yourself.

Suddenly you spot a bridge. It looks sturdy and well built and goes from your side to the other. The bridge leads to exactly where you want to go. Would you be annoyed and say, "Well, a bridge is fine, but I'm really more into parasailing. I think I should be able to parasail across. And what about people who want to try and pole vault? Why isn't it set up for that? I have a friend who likes to long jump—I think he should be able to do that too."

I can't imagine anyone wasting time with those thoughts. You'd probably just be thrilled that there *was* a way across—and you'd use it! But this is exactly what people say about the salvation God offers. "Who says there should only be one way to God? I think we should be able to find our own way, and all ways should be equally valid." These people are completely missing the point! Instead of being upset because God didn't consult them and provide several ways to him that meet with their approval, they should be rejoicing that he gave us an option at all!

Now for the second point—that Christianity is very exclusive and leaves lots of people out. I'm sorry, but that's just bull! Christianity is the most politically correct religion that has ever existed, and I'll show why.

Stay with the example of the bridge. Imagine yourself approaching it and seeing a sign on it. The sign says, "Anyone can use this bridge. You just have to step out on it, walk across it, and thank the builder who is waiting on the other side." Not too unreasonable, is it? After all, if you're going to use the bridge at some point, you have to walk across it. And it only seems correct to thank the person who built it. That's not exclusive at all.

On the other hand, imagine the sign saying, "This bridge may only be used by women from Costa Rica with red hair who are over six feet tall and who can turn cartwheels." That would be exclusive! Not many people would be able to qualify. But that's not what Christianity is like. God's love and salvation are available to *everyone*. None of the following matters:

- Race
- Gender
- Age
- Financial status
- Education level
- Political leanings
- Personality
- Talents
- Strength

All of these qualities are irrelevant when it comes to our standing with God. What he did (very wisely in my opinion!) is to put us all on an equal playing field. *Nothing* we can do earns us any points toward salvation. That means we all stand before God empty-handed and on exactly the same level. None of us have higher, or lower, standing before him.

This means we can choose to accept the gift of his son's death for our sins and be part of his family. We then live fulfilled, obedient, and active lives working for God's glory here on earth. When we die—well that's the best part by far! Let me just say that if your idea of heaven is floating on a cloud and playing a harp, you are *way* off base. Try to imagine your birthday, Christmas, Fourth of July, and every other fabulous holiday all rolled into one—you'll get a very faint idea of what is waiting for us. Heaven will be the best and most wonderful family reunion you can imagine, and we will be fully welcome in it. (For a really good idea of what it will be like, I strongly recommend the book *Heaven* by Randy Alcorn, Tyndale House, 2004.)

If we choose not to accept God's salvation (and he never forces anyone to do so), we live as best we can here on earth. But when we die, it's a completely different story. Hell will *not* be partying and hanging out with your friends. Hell will be terrible isolation, unimaginable pain, and unending regret. Everyone in hell will acknowledge Jesus as Lord over all, but for them it will be too late (Phil. 2:10 – "That at the name of Jesus every knee should bow, in heaven and on earth and under the earth,"). The thought of hell disturbs me, and I wish it didn't exist, but I know it does.

So the choice is up to you, and you'll never make a more important one in your life. If you have never prayed the prayer of salvation, my hope is that you'll take a minute and voice it now.

Grow in Godliness

Okay, hopefully you have prayed the prayer of salvation and are now a child of God—or have been one for some time but haven't gotten much past the starting point. Time for the next step:

Goal no. 2 – Learn about God's plan for your life and start becoming the person he wants you to be.

Although the *decision* to become one of God's children is a one-time thing, the *process* of becoming all he wants you to be is ongoing. You will never reach perfection here on earth, but if you start working on the following suggestions, you can begin moving closer to what God wants for you.

One of the best ways to find out about someone else is to spend time with them. Just think about a time when you met someone who really interested and attracted you. You probably sought them out, talked to them a lot, and looked for ways to spend time with them. That's exactly what you need to be doing with God now. Here are some suggestions for how to accomplish that.

1 – *Have a daily quiet time.* Sometimes this is called a devotional. You can do this at any time during the day although many people (myself included) prefer to do it in the morning. It gives you a good start to your day. What do I do in a quiet time, you ask? Good question and we'll go back to the above paragraph. When you've met someone who interests you, there is a desire to get to know them better. That is what a devotional time allows you to do with God. Here are some components to include:

- *Read his word* – The best way to find out about God is to read the Bible. It's like his letter to us. I suggest starting in the New Testament in one of the four Gospels—Matthew, Mark, Luke, or John. These tell about the life of Jesus when he was here on earth. In the Old Testament, try reading through Psalms and Proverbs. They both have excellent advice for living. There are lots of Bible reading plans available online or in Christian bookstores as well. Just find one that works for you.
- *Pray daily* – After you finish your scripture reading, talk to God. He wants us to do this! Tell him what's going on with you, seek out his help and direction, and ask him to help your friends and family. Years ago, my mom gave me a prayer guide called *ACTS* (also a book of the Bible I recommend!). It stands for the following:

- Adoration
- Confession
- Thanksgiving
- Supplication

It's a good guideline. You start out praising God, then confessing any sin in your life, thanking him for all the good things he has blessed you with, and then asking his help for you and others. I like it because it covers all the bases and is easy to remember. I've used it for years.

- *Put God's words in your heart* – Another tool I was given by Mom. She became a Christian in her twenties and was hugely influenced by the Navigators (a great Christian ministry based in Colorado Springs). One of the things they emphasize is memorizing scripture, and Mom did this her whole life. She got me started on the Navs Topical Memory System, which I still use today (I just went through some verses this morning). You can find it at any Christian bookstore or off the Navigator's Web site. More about this later.

2 – Find a biblical based church to attend on a regular basis. Do not make the mistake of thinking that you can be a Lone Ranger Christian. We are not designed that way. Yes, I've heard before that churches are full of hypocrites, but I consider that just an excuse to dodge doing something you know you need to do. Yes, churches are full of hypocrites—and liars, and cheaters, and fakers. In other words, churches are full of sinners. I consider that a good thing, or I'd never get to go into one since I'm a sinner myself—how about you? Be careful of expecting a perfect church (that's the black-and-white mentality many depressed individuals can have) because they don't exist. Look for a church where the following happens on a regular basis:

- *God's word is taught.* Do people pull out their Bibles and follow along while the preacher is talking? Is the Bible read from in worship services and small groups? Those are good signs. The point is not to learn what the preacher says but what *God* says.
- *You can form relationships with other people.* You want a place where people are warm and welcoming. It's really important to plug into a small group (sometimes called Sunday school groups) because if all you do is go to the service, it's easy to get lost in the crowd, especially in a large church.
- *There is great music.* I admit this is a personal must-have for me. I have always said that a good song speaks to me much more than a good sermon. I need to have a church with praise and worship style music rather than traditional hymns—although I do love some of the hymns as well.
- *You can find ways to serve and minister to others.* Look for a church that encourages its members to get involved. You don't want to just be a pew warmer. Look at what kind of ministries the church is involved in and try to find one that will use your talents. The more you put into a church, the more you'll get out of it.

3 – *Begin growing as a Christian.* This step is vitally important, and the Bible addresses it in several places (1 Peter 2:1–25, 1 Cor. 13:11, Heb. 5:12–14). Becoming a child of God is a great first move, but you don't want to stop there. Imagine a couple having a baby and how proud and excited they'd be. As good parents, they would encourage their baby to grow and develop. They would be somewhat concerned if several years later their child was still an infant—no matter how cute and cuddly! The point is that becoming a Christian is the first stage in an ongoing journey. It's not the end point. So here are some things you need to do if you haven't already.

- *Be baptized as a public demonstration of the decision you made.* The Bible is very clear that this is a necessary act of obedience for believers. It's a way for us to show the world the decision and commitment we have made. I've listed below a few scriptures that make reference to this.
  - Mark 16:16 – "Whoever believes and is baptized will be saved, but whoever does not believe will be condemned." (NIV)
  - Matthew 28:18–20 – "Then Jesus came to them and said, 'All authority in heaven and on earth has been given to me. Therefore go and make disciples of all nations, baptizing them in the name of the Father and of the Son and of the Holy Spirit, and teaching them to obey everything I have commanded you. And surely I am with you always, to the very end of the age.'" (NIV)

- Romans 6:3–6 – "Or don't you know that all of us who were baptized into Christ Jesus were baptized into his death? We were therefore buried with him through baptism into death in order that, just as Christ was raised from the dead through the glory of the Father, we too may live a new life." (NIV)

- *Tell others about your experience* – The Bible is very explicit about this as well. I've listed a few verses below that address this.

    - Matthew 5:16 – "In the same way, let your good deeds shine out for all to see, so that everyone will praise your heavenly Father." (NLT)

    - Romans 1:16 – "For I am not ashamed of this Good News about Christ. It is the power of God at work, saving everyone who believes— the Jew first and also the Gentile." (NLT)

    - Matthew 4:19 – "Jesus called out to them, 'Come, follow me, and I will show you how to fish for people!'" (NLT)

    - Matthew 16:15 –"And then he told them, 'Go into all the world and preach the Good News to everyone.'" (NLT)

As Christians we have been given an amazing gift—actually a whole set of gifts! Why wouldn't we want to share that with everyone we know. Think about a time when something good happened to you. Maybe you saw a great movie, found a fabulous sale, or heard a terrific song. What did you do? Most people, myself included, told others about it. That's a very natural reaction, and it's exactly what we should do about the gift of salvation we have been given. It's not something we should selfishly keep to ourselves.

- *Look for ministries to become involved in.* This is where we really start growing as a Christian, something I referred to earlier. Don't make the mistake of thinking that you have to be perfect before you start helping others. If that were the case, no one would be involved in ministries! One of the best ways to figure out where to plug in is to determine what your spiritual gifts are. If you are a new Christian, this may be a novel concept to you, so I'll explain.

When we accept God's gracious gift of salvation, we receive other gifts as well. All Christians have them and they are mentioned in the Bible in several different places (1 Corinthians 12, Romans 12, and Ephesians 4). If you are not sure what your spiritual gifts are, you need to find out. There are several SG tests and inventories available online. Pick a free one—you shouldn't have to pay. My favorite is *The Spiritual Gifts Analysis* on www.churchgrowth.org. I like that one because it's pretty comprehensive, and you'll be able to print out the results. When I taught at MACU, I had some of my classes take this because I think it's an important concept for every Christian to know.

Once you know your spiritual gifts, try to find a ministry to match them—you'll probably feel most comfortable and be most effective in those areas. For example, if you have the gift of mercy, you might do well comforting bereaved people. If you have the gift of hospitality, you might start reaching out to international students who are far from home. If you have the gift of administration, you might want to volunteer some time in your church office on a regular basis. The point is that if you match your gifts to the ministries you get involved in, you'll probably be more effective and will experience greater enjoyment.

A word of caution, however: we are all called occasionally to work outside of our area of giftedness. I personally do *not* have the gift of evangelism, but there have been times when I knew God was calling me to share the Gospel with someone, so I did. I wasn't as good as Billy Graham would have been (because he has this gift in spades!), but I did the best I could. Another example, when David and Josh were little and were in the church nursery, the policy was that all parents took a turn helping out there. I remember several parents claiming they shouldn't have to do this because they didn't have the gift of "working with young children." First, that isn't even a spiritual gift! Second, this is a perfect example of working outside your comfort zone due to an existing need.

Learn to Trust Him

O ne of the worst things about depression is that it can color all our perceptions and make it very easy to feel bad about everything. When you're right in the middle of a black cloud, it can be natural to believe that the entire world is a dark, miserable, dismal place. So here is your next goal:

> *Goal no. 3 – Remember, God is always there and always loves you, even if you can't feel him.*

Fortunately God is not bound by our awareness of him. When we feel hopeless, we tend to believe God is powerless. When we are in despair, we cannot imagine ever feeling his joy and love. When we are paralyzed by fear, it can be impossible to claim the freedom he offers.

This is when it's vitally important to know him and his promises well. When we have God's word in our hearts, we can make a deliberate choice to believe his assurances, in spite of the way we feel at the time. Here's how I visualize it. Imagine that your hometown has had several weeks of dark, stormy weather. Everyone is thoroughly sick of rain and gloom, and most people are feeling down. In spite of the fact that the sun hasn't made an appearance in weeks, we would all be pretty confident that it's still there. We would be able to state with assurance that even though we can't *feel* the sun, it continues to exist. We would act in faith on that—we wouldn't sell our shorts, flip flops, and bathing suits. We would know that eventually the sun would break through the clouds. The fact that we hadn't seen the sun in a while would not, in the least, detract from its continued existence.

It's the same with God. At times we walk through some very bleak and desolate experiences, and at those times we may not feel his presence. But we can't base God's reality on *our* emotional state. He exists outside and in spite of our perceptions. So at times, we just hang on tight to his promises and keep telling ourselves over and over that he will get us through it. We remind ourselves that God has *not* abandoned us. He is still there—strong, loving, and capable. He will never leave us or forsake us (Deuteronomy 31:8 – "The Lord himself goes before you and will be with you; He will never leave you nor forsake you. Do not be afraid; do not be discouraged." NIV).

The horrible, dismal times are when we need to cling to his promises even more tightly than normal. I heard a story once that really explains it well. A man was working on a small plane that had some ropes and cords dangling from it. (You need to suspend disbelief because the story is here to make a point. I have no idea if it's true or not although I suspect it isn't.) The plane took off, and somehow the man was tangled up in the ropes and cords and rose up in the air with the plane. By the time he was able to free himself, the plane was several hundred feet in the air. At this point, he was holding on the ropes as tightly as he could. The pilot realized what had happened and returned to the landing field. He brought the plane in (this is why I think this is not a true story—how would the plane land without killing the man?), and people came running over to help him. When they reached him, they had to literally pry his hands open. He had been clinging so tightly to the ropes that he couldn't unlock his fingers on his own.

This is what we need to do to God and his promises when we go through hard times. We need to cling to him so tightly that our hands have to be pried open. Unfortunately, however, most people *let go* instead of holding on. They become so discouraged they begin to believe God has abandoned them, and they walk away from his presence (and by the way, we always leave God—he never departs from us). This is understandable but not helpful. When I'm walking through a dark valley, I always visualize having a death grip on God's hand and his assurances. I don't want to fall!

Garbage In, Garbage Out

This next goal is related to what I was talking about in goal no. 3 and has to do with becoming discouraged and wandering away from God.

Goal no. 4 – Choose carefully the voices you listen to.

Have you ever seen the commercials where people have an angel perched on one shoulder and a devil on the other, both talking to them? I believe this is more accurate than we realize. Unfortunately, Satan is alive and well on planet Earth, and his goal is to mess our lives as much as possible. I addressed some of this in the "Things That Can Help – Mental" section, but it's important, so I want to address it again.

If you are not a Christian, you're living in Satan's territory. You're his to play with and control. If you're already a believer, he knows he's missed his big opportunity with you, but he's not done yet. Now he tries to undermine your confidence, misdirect, confuse, attack, and mire you down as much as possible. Spiritual warfare is anything Satan does to pull us away from God and his plan for our lives (my definition). At times it's active and overt, and other times it's very subtle and sneaky. The Bible addresses this very topic.

Ephesians 6:10–18 – Finally, be strong in the Lord and in his mighty power. Put on the full armor of God so that you can take your stand against the devil's schemes. For our struggle is not against flesh and blood, but against the rulers, against the authorities, against the powers of this dark world, and against the spiritual forces of evil in the heavenly realms. Therefore, put on the full armor of God so that when the day of evil comes, you may be able to stand your ground and, after you have done everything, to stand. Stand firm then, with the belt of truth buckled around your waist, with the breastplate of righteousness in place, and with your feet fitted with the readiness that comes from the gospel of peace. In addition to all this, take up the shield of faith, with which you can extinguish all the flaming arrows of the evil one. Take the helmet of salvation and the sword of the Spirit, which is the Word of God. And pray in the Spirit on all occasions with all kinds of prayers and requests. With this in mind, be alert and always keep on praying for all the saints (NIV).

We need to be prepared to defend ourselves against Satan's attacks, and our mindset needs to be *"when* the attacks come,"* not *if* they come. So be very aware of the voices in your head (and don't worry, we all have them!). If the voices are encouraging, positive, and strengthening, they're probably from God. They'll say things like the following:

- I know you can do it, for I am with you.
- You are good enough. I love you, and I made you.
- You are worthy of my love.
- I will be with you, and I will help you.

Regrettably, Satan is sending messages as well. They sound something like the following:

- You'll never be good enough.
- No one really likes you.
- They don't love you, and they'll all leave you alone.
- You aren't smart, capable, or strong enough.

It is *vital* to learn to recognize the voices talking to you and to figure out where they're coming from. Once you do that you can choose which one to listen and pay attention to. We can't do this on our own though. At times we are barraged by Satan's voices and his spiritual warfare. I've experienced this in my own life and have had to cry out to God and ask for his help because I was overwhelmed. When this happens, my prayer goes something like this:

Lord, I don't want to keep dwelling on these thoughts. I know they're not true or helpful. Please redirect my thoughts along the paths you want them to go. Remind me of your promises and help me get through this.

God honors these kinds of prayers. But as I've stated previously, at times I've prayed this twenty to thirty times in an hour! So learn to listen to the messages you're getting and figure out where they're coming from. I have a good example of this. I use Google for my main search engine and like it as my default home page on my computer. Somehow, another company has put themselves as my default home page, so every time I get online, it goes to them. I've tried everything I can to undo this (I don't think I did it in the first place!), but no matter what I do, whenever I get online, there is the other company.

This is exactly what Satan does. He keeps flipping us back to him. I don't know enough to fix my computer, and since it's relatively minor—Google is just one click away—I mostly just let it go. But in our lives, we have God as our super programmer (to stay with the example). Satan can be very persistent, but God is stronger, better, faster, and more capable. So if Satan is trying to reprogram your life, just keep asking God for his help. He is always there, and he'll listen. Remember that he loves you and wants you to stay on the right path.

Begin to Believe

We're almost done. There is one more very important thing you need to start doing to help you in your battle against the darkness that has been overtaking your life.

Goal no. 5 – Put God's word in your heart and choose to believe it even if you don't feel it.

If you are not in the habit of memorizing scripture, I encourage you to start. We all put things in our minds all the time, and it greatly influences how we act and feel. You may have heard the saying "Garbage in, garbage out." That's very accurate. If we fill our minds with worthless movies and TV programs or with dark, depressing thoughts, we will likely feel worthless and depressed. But if we put God's promises in our hearts, we will feel valued, worthwhile, and hopeful. There are lots of great verses to choose from. I'm putting in some of my favorites here.

- Romans 8:35–39 – "Who shall separate us from the love of Christ? Shall trouble or hardship or persecution or famine or nakedness or danger or sword? As it is written: 'For your sake we face death all day long; we are considered as sheep to be slaughtered.' No, in all these things we are more than conquerors through him who loved us. For I am convinced that neither death nor life, neither angels nor demons, neither the present nor the future, nor any powers, neither height nor *depth*, nor anything else in all creation, will be able to separate us from the love of God that is in Christ Jesus our Lord." (NIV)

- Jeremiah 29:11 – "'For I know the plans I have for you,' says the Lord. 'They are plans for good and not for disaster, to give you a future and a hope.'" (NLT)

- Matthew 11:28–29–"Come to me, all you who are weary and burdened, and I will give you rest. Take my yoke upon you and learn from me, for I am gentle and humble in heart, and you will find rest for your souls." (NIV)

- Philippians 4:19 – "And this same God who takes care of me will supply all your needs from his glorious riches, which have been given to us in Christ Jesus." (NLT)

- John 14:27 – "I am leaving you with a gift—peace of mind and heart. And the peace I give is a gift the world cannot give. So don't be troubled or afraid." (NLT)

- Isaiah 40:29–31 – "He gives power to the weak and strength to the powerless. Even youths will become weak and tired, and young men will fall in exhaustion. But those who trust in the Lord will find new strength. They will soar high on wings like eagles. They will run and not grow weary. They will walk and not faint." (NLT)
- Proverbs 1:33 – "But all who listen to me will live in peace, untroubled by fear of harm." (NLT)

One of the best things about the electronic age is that it is really easy to find things. So if you need verses on a particular topic, just go online and search for it. I do that all the time. Go to whatever search engine you use and type in something like, "Bible verses for overcoming fear, or obedience, or growing in God." The possibilities are endless. You can even find verses in different versions of the Bible. I like New International Version and New Living Translation. Find verses that speak to you in a translation you like and start memorizing them—you'll see a difference in your life!

What About Medication?

At some points, clients inevitably ask what I think about taking medication for depression. Usually they ask it hesitantly, as if expecting me to be horrified at the very idea. Here's my response, "I think that's a great idea! Let's try it and see if it helps."

In my opinion (and remember, I'm a PhD, not a medical doctor), medication for emotional conditions can be very beneficial, lifesaving even. To me, taking medicine for an emotional condition is no different than taking it for a physical one. Would you take meds for a heart condition, high blood pressure, or arthritis? Most people would answer yes without hesitation. But there is still some stigma attached to mental illness, and many people feel that if they're *just* depressed or anxious, they should be able to tough it out on their own.

This makes no sense to me. Medication is a perfectly good tool that hundreds of people have spent countless hours developing and perfecting—why not take advantage of that? Think of it this way. Let's say you've suffered from migraines for years, and they've become pretty debilitating. You have difficulty doing your job, socializing with friends, and enjoying your family. You go to a specialist who listens to your story and examines you. Then she tells you there's this wonderful pill that has been around for a few years. It works very well in cases like yours, and if you'll take a pill every day, your migraines should soon be a thing of the past. Would you respond, "Thanks, Doctor, but I really don't want to take any medicine. That seems like cheating—my family tells me if I'm strong enough, the migraines won't bother me. Besides if my friends knew I was taking pills for headaches, they'd all laugh at me." I hope none of you would!

I'll add here that Christians can be some of the worst offenders in this area. I've spoken to many good Christians who refuse meds because they are convinced it's unnecessary since God is going to heal them. I would never discount divine healing—I firmly believe it occurs. However, at times God heals us by directing us to the means he wants us to use. I believe medicine is an instrument God has given us to combat diseases and conditions that plague us. There's nothing wrong in taking it. Having said that, there are some things to take into account.

Never, ever, ever, ever (I know, it sounds like a Taylor Swift song!) take medication prescribed for someone else. That can be very dangerous and often causes more problems than it solves. You need to get a medication tailored for you, not someone else. Frequently clients don't know where to start looking for a prescription for antidepressants. Here are a few guidelines.

- If you're currently seeing a therapist for depression, ask them if they can refer you to someone. They may know of a doctor who specializes in this area.
- If you're not being treated for depression, call your family doctor and tell the person you talk to what you want. Your doctor may want to see you first, and that's fine. If they talk to you, they can get a better idea of how to help you. Some general MDs specialize in meds for emotional conditions, so they may prescribe something themselves. If not, they will probably refer you. If you aren't currently being treated for depression and don't have a family doctor, don't despair. There are other options—keep reading.
- Ask any health care professional you see on a regular basis—dentist, eye doctor, OBGYN, etc. Often they know who is in the area.
- Get online and Google (or whatever search engine you use) depression treatment in (wherever you live).
- Call a crisis hotline in your area. Let them know it's not an emergency but tell them what you're looking for. They often have a list of physicians who specialize in different areas.
- Ask a staff person at your church. They too often have lists of specialists.
- Check with your insurance company. They should be able to give you names of people who

treat depression and who are covered by your insurance plan.

- Check with your Human Resource Department at work. They also keep lists of specialists.
- Try to remember if you've heard any friends or acquaintances talk about being treated for emotional conditions. Ask them who they saw and how it worked out.

Okay, now you've gotten in to see a doctor who specializes in treating depression. They'll write you a prescription; you'll take the pills and be all well, right? Sorry, but it usually isn't that simple. We live in a society that wants instant answers—tomorrow would be good (yesterday would have been better!). Unfortunately, meds don't work quite that precisely. Getting the right medication for your particular condition can be a time-consuming, trial-and-error, and just plain frustrating process.

First, the doctor has to find the medication that works best for you. A lot enters into this. Your age, weight, gender, general health, other medications currently being taken, and family history to name a few. This can take a lot more time than the patient had been expecting. The correct drug has to be found, and the only way to do that is by educated trial and error. The doctor uses the information the patient has given him and makes a recommendation. Typically, several meds may be tried before finding one that works well. Then it's a matter of finding the correct dose. Things are further complicated if the patient is already on meds for other conditions.

The doctor has to make sure all the medications work well together.

So now you have seen a specialist and have a prescription for the antidepressant XYZ. Here are some guidelines to help you make sure you're on the right path.

- Take the meds as prescribed. Don't increase or decrease your dose without checking with your doctor first.
- Read up on your medicine and take notes of any side effects. If you experience any, call your doctor's office and let them know.
- Be patient! Usually drugs have to be taken for a certain amount of time before they take effect—sometimes a few weeks to a month.
- Be reasonable. If you're about a 30 on the RADS scale (see that chapter in the book), even the best antidepressants aren't going to get you to a 99 in a week. Going from a 30 to a 50 in a month is a big improvement and a more realistic expectation.

I have had depressed clients tell me that antidepressants literally saved their lives. So if you've been thinking about going this route, I would encourage you to give it a try. Just remember, there are no magic pills you can swallow and feel 100 percent better the next day. Find someone who can prescribe meds, take them as prescribed, be patient, and be realistic. You may find it makes a huge difference in how you act and feel!

A Word to Family and Friends

I've done my best to write a practical, helpful book for people who are suffering from depression. But some of you are in the same position I was, not depressed yourself but in a relationship with someone who is. I'm not sure which is harder—being the person who is so unhappy or experiencing the misery secondhand.

If you are not the primary sufferer, I do have some advice for you, but it may not be what you want to hear because there is no magic cure.

1. *You cannot fix the person who is depressed.* This is a tough one, especially if it's someone you love. But it's important you understand that healing this person's woes is not your job or responsibility. In fact, it's not even possible—it would be like trying to stop smoking for someone else. Some things

we have to do on our own, and recovering from depression is one of them.

2. *You do not have to keep their depression a secret.* If the depressed person is typical, they won't want anyone to know about it, and they will try to get you to agree to keep things undercover. The problem with this is if no one knows what's going on, they can't offer you support. Choose carefully whom you confide in, but do have a few people you can unburden to and who will offer you understanding and encouragement. Trust me when I say you'll need it!

3. *Don't allow the depression to excuse the person from doing what they need to do.* This one is tricky because there needs to be a balance between being kind and understanding and holding them accountable. Bottom line is we don't get many passes in life. It's very easy for the depressed person to say that they don't feel like going to their child's whatever (ball game, dance recital, spelling bee, etc.), and they probably don't. So you need to use your judgment here. Have they been to most functions, and has this been a tough week? If so, staying home and missing one event probably won't do much harm. But they can't establish a pattern of opting out of everything. It's not good for them or the family, and life does not stop for depression.

4. *Don't allow their depression to curb your enjoyment of life.* I always invited Ed to things, and especially in his last years, he almost always declined. I would usually go anyway, and at times I know he resented

it. After much thought, prayer, and discussion with friends and family who knew the situation, I decided that one victim to depression in the family was enough. So go to family functions, stay in touch with friends, take walks, and do whatever else you need to do (within reason!) to stay sane. You may be doing it alone, but this is the healthier path.

5. *Pray for them and you—regularly*! Often prayer feels like "just praying." But I can assure you it is much more than that. Pray for healing (in all areas) for the depressed person. Pray for strength and wisdom for yourself. Ask God to send some friends (other than you) who will be there for the depressed person, who will offer them encouragement, and who will hold them accountable.

6. *Hang in there*! Depression (especially major depression) is not easily or quickly overcome. Take care of yourself and remind yourself that this is a marathon, not a footrace. Recognize and celebrate small victories. Encourage the sufferer to make small changes and commend them for the baby steps they take. It does all add up, but it takes time.

7. *Be truthful with the kids, in small doses.* If the depressed person is your spouse and you have children at home, at some point the kids will notice what is going on with their depressed parent. They'll probably ask you at some time, "What's wrong with Mom/Dad? How come they never

want to do _____ anymore?" How much you say depends quite a bit on your child's age and maturity level. It will be a judgment call on your part as to what their level of understanding is. The best thing I can say here is never lie. Don't try to sugarcoat things. They'll figure it out eventually, and then, along with feeling let down by their other parent, they'll be mad at you for not telling the truth. Give them the truth in small bites. "Daddy is feeling sad right now" is a good beginning. It's okay to tell them to ask the other parent directly also. When you feel they're ready to handle it, schedule some time (preferably when you can be alone and uninterrupted) and tell them, "Mom has an illness called depression, and it makes it hard for her to do things." You're probably not telling them anything they don't already know, and I believe it's best to lay cards on the table. Answer any questions they may have and be as reassuring as possible.

8. *Take care of yourself.* I wish I could say otherwise, but on top of dealing with secondhand depression, you will probably still have to work, do household chores, cook, take the kids places, run errands, etc. You may end up taking on chores your partner is unable or unwilling to do. It's very easy to become resentful, angry, overwhelmed, frustrated, tearful, sad, etc., etc. I know because I experienced all of the above—sometimes all at once! Make time for yourself (and children, if you have any) to do fun things that you enjoy, with or without the

depressed person. Work out, connect with friends, get lots of sleep, eat well, and consider getting professional help. You need someone you can unload to periodically so you can stay sane.

Being in a relationship with a severely depressed person is never easy, and if that is where you are, you have my complete sympathy. Unfortunately I don't have a magic wand I can wave and fix everything; neither do you. Take things one day at a time and stay as positive as possible. Learn to enjoy the moment and try not to worry too much about the future. Improvement *can* happen, and you need to remind yourself of that—a lot!

Closing

This book has been written with much thought and prayer put into it. My main desire was to make something good come out of Ed's life. His last years on earth were miserable and wretched due to his overwhelming depression. But at heart, he was a kind, loving, and funny man. Sadly, all his good qualities got swallowed up by the darkness that came to dominate his life.

David, Josh, and I all know, without a trace of doubt, that Ed is in heaven now and is currently full of joy, reveling in unimaginable fellowship with Jesus and reconnecting delightedly with friends and family. We are enormously happy for him although we wish he could have found some of that contentment here on earth.

My hope for you is that you will use this book and the tools provided in it to improve your life now. That you will be able to push back the darkness of depression and reclaim your life. That you will reunite with family and friends, be able to cope better with work or school, and strengthen your relationship with God.

Please remember that while you may not have asked for the depression you are experiencing, and done nothing to deserve it, you are the only one who can make it better. My prayer is that you will, with God's help, find the strength to make needed changes. Keep in mind that God loves you more than you can ever imagine or understand, and he is always just a prayer away.

Pushing Back the Darkness Workbook

S o you've read the book and realized that you saw yourself throughout its pages. You know you suffer from depression and, hopefully, would like to change that. How do you go about it?

Overcoming depression is possible, but you need to understand that this will likely be a long-term project. Many of you have been miserable for years, and you simply aren't going to be significantly better in a few weeks, as much as you might want to be. I often tell clients that I don't have a magic wand, but if I did, I would be happy to wave it and fix all your problems. You don't have a magic wand either, but you do have your determination and this workbook as a guideline. You'll see that the workbook has enough pages to record twelve months. If you have been depressed for several years, you will need to record in the workbook until it's *full*—as a minimum. I know it sounds like a lot, but remember the saying, "Rome wasn't built in a day"? It's absolutely true.

The more you fill out these pages on a *daily* basis, the sooner you will feel better. I stress doing this for a year because I've seen that depressed individuals have two tendencies when working to get better:

- They put in effort for a little while (usually a few days), and, when they're not 100 percent better, they stop trying,
- They try for a few days and start feeling a little better—and stop doing the things that improved their situation!

Neither of these things is helpful. You need *sustained effort over time*, done *consistently* to obtain the results you want. Remember the weight loss examples? To lose one hundred pounds, you need to eat better and exercise more for several months to over a year. It won't happen in a few days or weeks.

A quick note of explanation: a positive action is just what it sounds like. Something you did (even if you didn't feel like it) where you gained a sense of accomplishment. Some examples are taking the dog for a walk, weeding the flower bed, baking cookies with your child, washing and cleaning out your car, balancing your checkbook, fixing a leaky faucet, doing laundry, going through your clothes and sorting out the ones you no longer use, playing catch with your child, etc. Anything where you can look back and feel like you took action instead of just sitting around (especially if sitting around was what you really felt like doing).

So take a few minutes and fill out a page (actually half a page) every day. Commit to doing it *daily*. Please remember to date each page because this will allow you to look back and see your progress. You might also note what number you are on the RADS scale *before* doing a few of the items and how you feel *after* doing them. Hopefully your score will be a little higher after exercising, taking a positive action, etc. Remember, even a few points here and there add up over time!

Rich Assessment of Depression Scale (RADS)

On a scale of 1–100, identify where you are right now. Use the following examples as guidelines (you may be a 55 or a 47—go with what feels right to you). There is some overlap in the numbers of the scale. This is deliberate because your score will be your best estimate, not a precise number.

100–90
You display excellent functioning in most, to all, areas of life. Issues are handled well and seldom, if ever, seem unmanageable. You have a wide range of resources that you use to deal with problems. Others tend to seek your advice and company because of your confident approach and upbeat attitude. No depressive symptoms.

90–80

You function very well in all life areas. You are socially active and have a wide range of interests and activities. In general you are satisfied and content with your life. You take pleasure in the company of your friends and family, function well in your job (or school, retirement, or other main interest), and enjoy hobbies and/or recreational activities during your free time. Problems are dealt with quickly and usually do not get blown out of proportion. Absent or very mild and temporary depressive symptoms.

80–70

If depressive symptoms are present, they are temporary and predictable reactions to life stressors (e.g., feeling sad when a friend or family member moves away). Only mild difficulties in overall functioning are present (e.g., some problems in concentration, turning school or work assignments in slightly late). You are not greatly concerned about this, however, because you understand what is causing your symptoms and believe things will improve with time. You are confident that family and/or friends will be present to help you work your way through any given situation. Temporary, minor depressive symptoms.

70–60

You have some slight depressive symptoms (e.g., loss of concentration or loss of appetite) *or* minor problems dealing with normal everyday situations (e.g., difficulty sleeping, lack of focus at work or school), but generally you cope well and have some strong personal relationships you rely on. Overall you deal with problems in a competent manner and are able to function well in most situations. Minor depressive symptoms.

60–50

You experience mild to moderate depressive symptoms somewhat frequently but, for the most part, are able to function fairly well in spite of them. You may have some extremes in symptoms (e.g., poor appetite or overeating, difficulty sleeping or sleeping much more than usual). You are beginning to have some difficulty in social, work, or school functioning (e.g., few friends, conflicts with peers or coworkers). For the most part, you are able to hide your symptoms from everyone except close family. You don't understand why you feel the way you do and are beginning to be alarmed about it. Mild to moderate depressive symptoms.

50–40

Your depressive symptoms have become more frequent and serious and are starting to impact your life in a negative way. You experience low energy and feel tired most of the time. You have a low self-esteem and have a difficult time making decisions. You are still able to function fairly well in work or school, but mistakes due to lack of concentration and/or indecisiveness are becoming more common and harder to hide. When you do get home, you feel drained of all vitality. What you feel like doing is sitting in a dark room and staring at a wall. Summoning up the energy to interact with family members can seem like an overwhelming task. Moderate depressive symptoms.

40–30

Your depression has become more severe and more frequent. There are very few times when you do not feel sad, blue, or despondent. You are still able to function in some areas of your life (e.g., working or going to church), but doing so is extremely difficult for you. You call in sick frequently to work or school and find it very difficult to interact with other people. They get on your nerves, and you wish everyone would leave you alone. Any social function requires enormous effort and rarely seems worth the trouble. You likely have gained or lost a significant amount of weight. You cry or feel like crying often. Moderate to severe depressive symptoms.

30–20

You are very depressed most days and have been this way for some time. You may still be able to function in a few areas of life (e.g., holding down a job or maintaining relationships with family or friends), but these activities require a tremendous effort on your part. Consequently, you feel exhausted most of the time. Your normal activities no longer bring you pleasure—in fact, there is very little in life that you enjoy. You are concerned about flunking out of school or losing your job because of your frequent absences or mistakes. Severe depressive symptoms.

20–10

You are extremely depressed most of the time and have great difficulty functioning because of the severity and duration of your depressive symptoms. You feel hopeless most of the time—you are beginning to believe that things will always be this way for you, and you are beginning to question whether you should continue living. You feel either very restless or very lethargic. Extremely severe depressive symptoms.

10–0

Your depressive symptoms are massive and ever-present—they have totally taken over your life. You either have attempted suicide or are seriously contemplating it. You are convinced that things will never improve for you and believe your friends and family would be better off without you. You are unable to function in vocational or social situations. You rarely leave your home and have little contact with anyone except family. Critically severe depressive symptoms.

Date _____
RADS score (lowest and highest for day) _____

I did the following items today (check all that apply)

- Had a devotional _____
- Grooming (took a shower or bath, brushed my teeth, combed my hair, put on fresh clothes, etc.)_____
- Tidied up my room or house_____
- Exercised (what and how long) _____
- Interacted with other people_____
- Got out of the house for a while_____
- Said my positive affirmations _____

I am grateful for (3 things) _____
A positive action I took today was _____

The following should be done at least once a week:

- Something new I tried today was_____
  _____
- I helped someone by_____
  _____
- Something fun I did today was_____
  _____
- Today I got together with (family member or friend)_____ and did _____
  _____
- Today I de-cluttered the following area in my home _____

Date _____
RADS score (lowest and highest for day) _____

I did the following items today (check all that apply)

- Had a devotional _____
- Grooming (took a shower or bath, brushed my teeth, combed my hair, put on fresh clothes, etc.)_____
- Tidied up my room or house_____
- Exercised (what and how long) _____
- Interacted with other people_____
- Got out of the house for a while_____
- Said my positive affirmations _____

I am grateful for (3 things) _____
A positive action I took today was _____

The following should be done at least once a week:

- Something new I tried today was_____
  _____

- I helped someone by_____
  _____

- Something fun I did today was_____
  _____

- Today I got together with (family member or friend)_____ and did _____
  _____

- Today I de-cluttered the following area in my home _____

Appendix

Positive Affirmations for Depression

Please note that this is a starter, general list. As you think of others, feel free to add them, or to tweak the ones that are here to make them more applicable to your situation. Just make sure they're worded in a positive manner and not a negative one.

I'll give an example to show what I mean.

Don't say–I will not think negative thoughts.

Instead say–I will avoid negative thoughts.

Evidence suggests that wording affirmations in the positive makes them much stronger and more powerful.

Repeat this list to yourself several times a day. Don't worry if what you're saying isn't true right now. You're saying things about the person you're *becoming*, not necessarily the person you are currently.

- I am an enthusiastic and upbeat person.
- I avoid making judgments of myself and others.
- I am aware of beauty all around me.
- I am free from depression forever.
- I have an enthusiastic outlook on life.
- I am happy and fulfilled.
- I embrace positive self-esteem.
- I avoid giving into depression.
- I pursue my life's purpose with confidence and enthusiasm.
- I only have positive thoughts.
- My life is full of joy!
- I express the joy of living. I allow myself to enjoy every moment of every day totally.
- Happiness is a state of mind and it is *my* state of mind.
- I choose to be happy!
- My possibilities are endless!
- I easily release the negative things in my life.
- My glass is more than half full. My life is overflowing with goodness.
- I love my life!
- I smile when I see people because happiness is contagious.
- I love myself. I am safe and secure.
- I have positive expectations and excited anticipation in life.
- I deserve to have a wonderful life.
- I am at peace.
- I let go of painful things in my past and move forward to my happy future.

- I feel joyful and excited about my life!
- Every day good things come to me.
- Joy and ease are familiar to me.
- I forgive and let go of the past and move into joy.
- I find it easy to stay positive
- I only focus on the positive things in life.
- I am free from negative thoughts.
- I like and accept myself just as I am.
- I am good enough.
- I deserve nice things in my life.
- I will continue to banish depression from my life.
- Every day I feel happier and better.
- I am a strong, capable person.
- I am free of negative thoughts.
- I will focus on the positive.
- I am learning to love and accept myself.
- I am becoming a positive thinker.
- I enjoy my life to the fullest.
- People see me as a happy, content person.
- Others enjoy being around me.
- I avoid dwelling on negative things in my past or present.